CW00751227

THE

BOOK OF

STICKS

Ancient & Modern

By
Alun Rees

Copyright © Alun Rees 2018
Illustrations © Talking Stick Books LLC 2018

All rights reserved. No part of this book may be reproduced in any form or by
electronic or mechanised means including information storage and retrieval
systems – except in the form of brief quotations embodied in critical articles or
reviews – without express permission in writing from the publisher.

Published by

TALKING STICK BOOKS LLC
66 S. Village Rd
Westmoreland, New Hampshire 03467

USA.
Office (866) 994-7539
UK
01672288749

www.talkingstickbooks.com

ISBN-13: 978-0-9991719-4-3
ISBN-10: 0-9991719-4-1

THE WONDER OF STICKS

There's something reassuring about the feel of a good stick, call it a staff or stave if you will, fitting closely in the grip of your hand. It's as if by instinct you know it will help guide you across the land and protect you from the dangers of the day and the threats of the night. Just looking at its polished patina and the discreet blade marks where it's knots and curves have been 'dressed' by the craft worker tells you it is no longer a mere branch of wood. Instead it has metamorphosed into an inert companion; a thing of useful beauty. Chosen to match hand and stride it becomes a trusted friend and, if you think about it, that should be no surprise.

Our earliest ancestors used sticks as their first technology to hunt for food and as kindling to conjure fire for the campsite. They were our first weapons too so sticks are hard-wired into the deep recesses of our species memory. As time swam on we used them as the simplest calculators, counting for us with small cuts on a tally stick. Our first music was made with a stick too and if someone hadn't picked one up to beat in time on a hollow log where would we be for rhythm?

Over the millennia humans have had a close and constant relationship with sticks in a myriad forms and guises employing them in cooking and cuisine, in medicine and construction; in agriculture and industry and sadly for torture and punishment too.

They are cultural icons and sporting implements; batons of insignia for chiefs and military leaders, talking sticks and hockey sticks. They are the source of myths, fables and proverbs and the font of magic be it from the magician's wand or conjured from an orchestra mimicking the moves of the conductor's baton in sound.

We use sticks to measure the pace of soldiers' marching, sticks to swagger with and sticks to weave with. We name places after them as they range across a vast spectrum of uses, literally from Pooh Sticks to poo sticks. In temperate climates we favour yew, blackthorn, apple wood, ash, cherry, holly and hazel but the world throws up so many types of wood suitable for a bewildering number of uses that the list grows long and exotic.

As I write spring is running into summer and the by-ways and footpaths of rural Britain are being engulfed by a surge of rampant growth. Those wishing to follow the paths have to navigate through seas of bracken, cow parsley and high seeding grasses...and nettles of course, always plenty of stinging nettles. That's why I carry a stick with me on my daily forays into the forest and on my strolls along the riverbank. I use my stick to 'beat a path'. Overhanging nettles are beheaded and I drive back tick-bearing bracken to allow my safe passage.

I've always carried a stick with me in the countryside and I remember my grandfather's stricture, telling me that anyone who doesn't is a complete fool. "How are you going to fight off a bear or trap an adder if you haven't got a stick?" he'd tell me gruffly as though my life depended on it.

I believed him. Still do. And my stick is never far away from me. If through some calamity I lose a stick the sense of loss nags me for weeks while I try to love the replacement. My favourites are thumb sticks with their V-shaped heads, allowing me a comfortable grip as I steady myself on rough terrain. And I can use it to compress the top strand of barbed wire to swing my leg over a fence. Since my children have grown up I've favoured a shorter stick, about three feet long, but when they were little I would use a shoulder length thumb stick to steady myself as one or other of them travelled in an infant backpack on my shoulders as we strode over the Marlborough Downs in Wiltshire. I still have wistful memories of my eldest son Harry gnawing at the stick as I held it up for him to teethe on it.

My daughter Alice, not yet able to walk, sat high and curious, looking over my shoulder. She'd insist on holding my stick with a hand so tiny it could only grasp one tine of the V as she listened to the chime of it's brass ferrule bouncing off the stones on our chalky path. Every few yards the stick would spring from her hand against a flint. I'd pick it up and she would demand it back again with outstretched hand and I'd oblige; it was truly a joystick. It was different with my youngest Morgan. He wasn't too interested in the backpack days but had a later introduction to sticks, which I would hurl after him as he ran laughing down forest rides when he'd given me some cheek. That's how he learnt to stay on his toes.

So, whilst beating a path through the undergrowth in the forest near my Wiltshire home, I thought of these things and wondered. Why not celebrate the not-so-humble stick I thought. I decided to write this book as a tribute knowing at the outset I'd need a forest of paper to do the subject of sticks true justice and that I could never do. Why not try though? Little did I realise what a Pandora's Box would open when I started to research the subject. Sticks are everywhere in human history and even in today's technologically advanced world many cultures still rely on them for their essential needs.

For nearly fifty years I've been a journalist working for British national newspapers covering murder and mayhem as a news correspondent and there are some stick stories from my assignments included in these pages. I've also drawn on memories and recollections of stick adventures with family and friends and woven them into the basketry of this collection. These anecdotes stand as motifs for the tone of this book encompassing as they do the curious, the amusing and the downright astonishing,

In these pages I also make some assertions and proffer a few theories about subjects that sticks have thrown up during the course of my life and through my research. They're all my own opinions garnered through the employment of whatever critical thinking I'm capable of mustering so please feel free to disagree. I shan't mind. I've tried to be as factually accurate as possible so forgive me any inaccuracies, as this is very much a story of sticks rather than a concise history. And forgive me too for any momentous stick stories I may have overlooked, after all there are so many. But one thing's for certain, sticks and stones may break your bones but these words of mine can never hurt you.

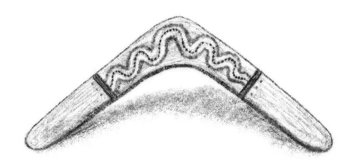

Chapter 1
THE STICK AGE

It's an awful scene. One of our hominid ancestors, an early ape-like human, picks up a long femur from a pile of bones and turns it in his hand while he contemplates the possibilities. His eyes narrow and our long, long distant forbear has a moment of realisation. With shrieks of triumph he carries his bone cudgel into battle; using it to brain a rival clan leader. What I've just described is, of course, the opening sequence of Stanley Kubrick's *2001: A Space Odyssey*. But hold on a minute. Cut! A bone Stanley? Surely not a bone, though I can see the powerful symbolism. No, far more likely our ancient and earliest forbears used a stick on the day they chose to weaponize themselves.

Spears very quickly followed clubs and for a clue has to how that happened, we need look no further than a clan of Western Apes living near Kedougou in Senegal, Africa. They make their own spears specifically for hunting and have been observed to break straight limbs off trees and strip away any side shoots and bark before sharpening one end with their teeth. Their quarry are the galagos or bush babies that sleep in deep hollows in trees where the apes can't reach unless they spear them and drag them out. Interestingly they toss their implements aside when the hunt is over. How long, I wonder, before they develop the desire to keep a prized spear that fits the palm? Shades of a different movie I think; *The Planet of the Apes* perhaps.

Time moved on and there are examples of simple wooden spears used by humans around 420,000 years ago and with that must have come the discernment not yet achieved by the Western Apes; different sticks for different uses. The best wood for prized clubs and spears; the rest dried out for the fire and maybe that's been happening for around 600,000 years since early man is thought to have first mastered the control of flames. Oh, and by the way the ancients often created sparks by using friction from a stick spun round by a bow drill to make the sparks and embers that started their fires. No sticks. No fire. Ray Mears and generations of modern survival buffs haven't bettered that method, which they consider to be a right of woodcraft passage.

At this point, though I'm only an amateur historian, it's worth giving you a brief overview of the pre-history of mankind to give our sticks a context. As we developed into the species we are today, breeding out and culling rival Neanderthals on our way, we developed various technologies. Archaeologists use them to delineate the different 'Ages' of modern man. We start with the Stone Age, which is split into three distinct periods. The first two are the Palaeolithic and the Mesolithic, which began over two and a half million years ago and encompass the eras of our very earliest ancestors up to modern man. These are mind numbingly immense lengths of time and are characterised by the rather esoteric categories of worked stone tools those people used. Specialist archaeologists devote their lives to identifying these implements, many of which would be indistinguishable from building rubble to the untutored eye.

The last period of the Stone Age is the Neolithic and in the Northern Hemisphere that more or less coincides with the retreating glaciers at the end of the last Ice Age some twelve thousand years ago. It's around this time that things really began to kick off as technology, whilst not exactly in a state of white heat, was developing at a faster pace. The use of finer stone tools called microliths concurrent with the arrival of metal on the scene. Hence we have the well-known Bronze Age, which overlapped the Neolithic and ran up to the arrival of the Iron Age some three thousand years ago in the Middle East and a little later in Europe. In fact before either of those two famous metal ages there was the less familiar Copper Age too. Archaeologists call it the Chalcolithic, a relatively short period when copper was used on its own before it was discovered the addition of a little tin to the mix created the harder and more durable alloy bronze

The one constant throughout all these early stages of technology was the stick. We'd been using smooth stones as simple hand clubs too but they imposed the need to get very close to bucking, kicking, biting quarry. However when you fix your stone to a length of wood it means you can stand back a little and take advantage of the far greater kinetic power at the end of its swing. Our forbears had also learnt longer sticks could be sharpened and have their points hardened in the fire.

This made it possible to throw them at fleeing prey from a distance or to hold more fearsome quarry at bay. In time, someone had the bright idea of using a short length of stick to use the principle of leverage and throw a spear even further; these spear throwers are known as atlatls.

It was around two hundred thousand years ago that early man discovered how to combine stick and stone technology. They found that carefully napped stone points, flint was a favourite, could be fitted onto the end of their spears giving them greater penetration than those fire-hardened points, which often snapped on impact. When bow and arrow technology became more sophisticated we already knew what we had to do and we fastened our flaked stone points onto the sharpened wooden sticks we used as arrows to give them even greater striking power.

The incorporation of wood with stone throughout these early ages of technology depended on a technique called hafting. It's recognised as a highly significant step in mankind's development involving complex processes and arguably marks the point where we became toolmakers in a very real sense. Put simply hafting is the skill of securely fastening a stone or metal point to a stick projectile. This usually involves creating flanges or indentations at the end of a stick to attach the sharp point or edge needed to construct a spear or arrow and later an axe. The stick part of the assembly usually has some sort of a 'plug' to accept the head, which is then bonded with glue made from resin and twine made from animal tendons. Hafting is a big subject and even today in the Age of Superglue there are quirky enthusiasts who practice its techniques just for the pleasure of doing so.

You see the point though. Without the stick how could our species have delivered their Stone, Bronze or Iron Age hunting technology successfully? They could have flaked and napped stone arrowheads and spearheads till the mammoths came home but without their stick delivery system they were going nowhere. So I unilaterally declare the Stick Age, the technological period that encompasses the Stone Age, the Copper Age, the Bronze Age and the Iron Age too. However my declaration of a Stick Age requires I confront the intrinsic problem with wood in archaeology.

Essentially relatively little wood survives in comparison with stone or metal and this means wood does not enjoy the recognition I believe it deserves. Britain's most famous prehistoric site at Stonehenge, for example, survived the ravages of time relatively well to remain a place of pilgrimage to this day. On the other hand, the giant standing timbers of Woodhenge, just three miles away, succumbed to insects and weather. Where the wooden uprights once stood in a complex pattern we now only have their post-holes in the ground like the roots of rotten teeth. That doesn't make Woodhenge unimportant, far from it, but it does make it invisible except in artist's impressions and our own imaginations. Out of sight out of mind, as the saying goes.

Wood, together with other organic materials like leather and textiles, is best preserved in wet or boggy sites where anaerobic conditions hostile to microbial action naturally occur. No microbes, no rotting. In 1970 on the Somerset Levels near Glastonbury a peat digger called Ray Sweet discovered a one-mile stretch of raised wooden causeway, which at six thousand years old, is the world's oldest known purpose-built thoroughfare. It's called the Sweet Way in honour of Ray. It follows then that archaeologists working on wetland sites will find a great deal of preserved material that would otherwise have decomposed. At sites in Ireland, Britain and Denmark for instance the bodies of human sacrifices, executed then thrown into bogs, have been discovered. They were so well pickled by thousands of years immersed in slightly acid water they yielded all sorts of information under the microscope. Everything from their tattoos to the last meals they ate, even their hair gel, has been revealed because of the extraordinary level of preservation.

Similarly the Ozette site in Washington State on the west coast of the USA was home to a pristine Native American settlement, which was destroyed by a massive mudslide. Unluckily for the villagers but fortunately for posterity the mud was an anaerobic deluge and it preserved a snapshot of Stick Age culture with fishing spears, bows and arrows, long houses and baskets, which after all are woven sticks. Ozette had been a village of the Makah Tribe of Native Americans who were and still are a skilled whaling and fishing people. Harpoons were found under the mudslide too; the sticks that Makah heroes used to hunt the giants of the deep.

Conversely the trouble with relatively dry locations is that insects and microbes combine to render wood into strata resembling potting compost mixed in amongst the stone or metal that mankind had used in conjunction. All that seems to have worked against the reputation of wood and it being duly accorded the recognition it deserves because sticks have been essential to everyday life in a fundamental way that modern people, including myself, are too cosseted to properly appreciate.

A couple of ancient individuals also stand as testament to the Stick Age and I'd like to evoke them here. The first is a very famous man indeed. He's the Pharaoh Tutankhamen, who ruled Egypt three thousand three hundred years ago. King Tut was a man who had a collection of wonderful bows and spears among the six thousand grave goods stacked in his tomb. But the young king also had six wonderful chariots buried with him in case he ever wanted to take a spin around his kingdom in the after world. The point is the chariots relied on the latest stick technology of the time in the form of wheel spokes that made them lightweight and highly manoeuverable war machines. In a subsequent chapter I'll come to the story of other sticks that underpinned the entire culture of the Pharaohs and quite literally symbolized their power.

The second individual is not so famous and died around five thousand five hundred years ago. That's long before King Tut walked the earth but he's no less eloquent for that and his name is Otzi the Iceman whose frozen body was discovered in a melting glacier on the Austrian/Italian border in 1991. It was an anaerobic sort of place that preserved his remains for forensic examinations that paint a picture of a man in his forties, desperate and on the run. Already wounded in the shoulder Otzi was suddenly shot in the back with an arrow as he made his way over a Tyrolean mountain pass. It was a fatal wound in a murder that remained undiscovered for millennia. Thanks to science we know a lot about Otzi. We know, for example, he had suffered a daunting array of illnesses ranging from Lyme Disease to parasitic worms. We also know that he was local to the Tyrol and that his last meal was a very fatty mixture of venison and the meat of an Ibex, a type of wild Alpine goat, along with some seeds and grains.

But what interests me most about Otzi is the kit he was carrying. His most prized possession appears to have been an axe with a copper head and a yew handle, which curved over like a swan's neck to hold the hafted axe-head pointing down like a beak; hence these are called 'swan beak' axes. His knife had a blade made of chert, a kind of silicon rock with properties similar to flint, and was mounted on a handle made of ash. He had a quiver containing fourteen arrows made from viburnum and dogwood, though only two of them were fletched with stabilising fins at the end. The same two were also the only ones actually fitted with flint arrowheads; the rest were unfinished. Otzi was also carrying a longbow made of yew that measured seventy- two inches in length. Like the arrows it was unfinished and had not yet been bent to shape, a process which usually involved steaming the wood first. The string for the finished bow was in the quiver ready for fitting.

It seems unlikely that under normal circumstances Otzi would have ventured onto the slopes of the mountain with a bow that didn't work and arrows that couldn't be shot. After all, the area was home to wolves, bears and wildcats. There's been some speculation that he was killed in a battle between warring clans but I don't think so. He was ten thousand feet above sea level. Why would clans climb so high for a violent punch-up? They'd be completely knackered before they could set too. And anyway Otzi had weapons that weren't in working order. What warrior in his right mind would trudge up a mountainside to go into battle with a bow he couldn't pull and arrows that wouldn't fire?

No, I think it was more personal than that. I reckon Otzi only risked venturing onto such a high pass without proper defences because he was fleeing from someone. It suggests to me that he had to leave an encampment or village in a hurry and he already had a shoulder wound from a previous fight. The question I pose is this, was Otzi a murderer or a thief or had he made free with someone's wife or daughter? We'll never know but we do know that he didn't cast aside his bow even though it wasn't fit for purpose. I think he was grateful to have that six-foot long yew stick, which reverted to use as a staff to help him on his headlong flight up the mountain. Unfortunately for Otzi it was not enough, and someone caught up with him and killed him with an arrow fired into his rib cage severing a main artery so that he bled out.

Whatever else he may have been, Otzi was a man who lived on the cusp between the Neolithic and the Chalcolithic. He lived at a time when stone technology was giving way to metal. That process would continue for many centuries as our ancestors maintained some reliance on stone tools while discovering, testing and perfecting metals like bronze and iron. Sticks though, in all their guises, remained central and vital to the production of tools for hunting, warfare, forestry, emerging agriculture and house building. Otzi's story embodies the Stick Age.

I remember one personal and very instructive introduction to another ancient and transformative stick in the curved, flat, aerofoil form of a boomerang; the iconic hunting weapon of the Australian Aboriginals. Quite how someone discovered that such an object can be thrown and then return is beyond me although I suspect it may have involved an absent minded chuck followed by a blow on the back of the head.

My introduction came when Harry, my eldest child, was about nine or ten years old and my great friend John Hounslow, who is a river keeper on the local chalk stream, brought one back as a present from a trip Down Under. Harry and I decided we'd give it a go and went to Marlborough Common for the launch although I have to say I was pretty sceptical about the homing powers of the boomerang. It was a windy day and I threw it with a flick of my wrist and watched in fascination as it caught the breeze and began to pulse through the air with a rhythmic, whooshing sound. Higher and higher it went pulling at the sky with unexpected and daunting power until I noticed it had reached a turning point, the zenith of its elliptical flight, and began to head straight back towards us.

I'm not faint-hearted but this Creature of Stick was almost howling on its return and I was gripped by an entirely rational terror, believing it was quite capable of beheading my beloved son. I grabbed Harry's hand and ran, perhaps the correct term is fled, headlong away from the technically returning, but actually pursuing, boomerang until it struck the ground behind us with a thud that shook the Common. No prizes for guessing the boomerang has been grounded ever since and from time to time I ponder whether I should lock it in an ebony box to protect future generations. Harry remembers the pulsing menace of that boomerang to this day and when I reminded John of his gift he told me, "That wasn't a tourist souvenir Al, I bought it from an Aboriginal guy who makes them the old way. It was the real thing."

"No kidding John," I sighed, "I knew that the moment I threw the bloody thing into the wind."

An Australian icon then the boomerang and there are archaeological records of them, and the non-returning throw stick known as a kylie or shaunie, on fifty thousand year old Aboriginal rock art depicting bird hunts and a kangaroo being clobbered. Actual specimen boomerangs believed to be ten thousand years old have been found in the Outback too but if you want to find the oldest known boomerang in the world then make the unlikely trip to Poland where a thirty thousand year old original was found in a cave in the Carpathian Mountains. They've been found in the Netherlands, India, the Middle East and North America too, which goes to show that more than one person in more than one location can independently have the same good stick idea.

These days our modern weapons are largely based on tube or barrel technology through which projectiles, either bullets or shells, are fired. But the origins of these modern weapons lie with a prototype stick technology too. Dart firing blowguns have been around for millennia and indeed are still favoured by those tribal cultures clinging to existence deep in the forests of the Amazon or New Guinea. Essentially blowguns (we used to call them blowpipes when I was a kid but apparently that's more to do with glass blowing) are hollow tubes quite often made from bamboo or similar cane-like plants with soft, pithy centres that can be removed.

Blowguns can be anything from eighteen inches to more than twenty feet in length depending on geography and purpose. They are not thought to have been much use for warfare, despite some of the better scenes from the Indiana Jones movies, but they're excellent for hunting small mammals and birds. Quite often the tips of the darts are dipped in disabling poisons like curare to bring down larger prey such as monkeys.

I owned a sort of blowgun myself many years ago though we called it a peashooter and like many young boys I found it essential equipment for tormenting anyone sitting in front of me in class. In those school days of mine I would have loved the thought of a poison dip for my peas although I have a less lethal frame of mind these days. Like me the Aztecs of Mexico liked to use blowguns for hunting too and there are some ceramic pots which show typically grisly scenes of human sacrifice also show the butchers, complete with beak masks, taking a break from heart-tearing duties to enjoy a blowgun hunt. More of the Aztecs later.

There's another thing about the Stick Age that piques my curiosity. As mankind was developing new tools from stone and metal incorporated with sticks, he was also striking up a relationship with dogs as hunting partners around fourteen thousand years ago.

Some scientists believe this partnership is what gave mankind extra cognitive power. Perhaps when dogs took on the role of scenting out our quarry for us we were able to reduce the size of the olfactory centres of our own brains and free up neurological resources for other tasks. Essentially that meant less smelling, more thinking.

Over millennia our canine friends developed into the mind-boggling number of breeds we now have but here's the burning question. Who first thought of throwing a stick for a dog? Whoever it was made them into enthusiastic retrievers and I think I know the answer. We'll come back to it.

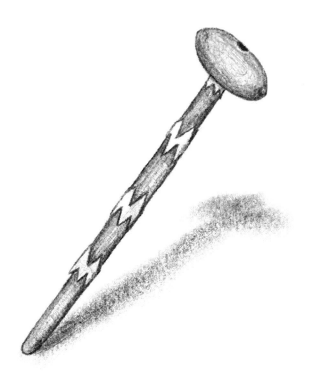

Chapter 2
STICK POWER

He was a giant of a man, the chief they laid to rest in Bush Barrow, a burial mound within sight of Stonehenge, six feet tall at a time when most people were five foot two. So special and powerful was he they buried his corpse intact when the custom was to cremate the dead or offer them to the excoriating kites and ravens in sky burials. With him were buried some of the most astonishing Bronze Age artefacts ever found on mainland Britain. 'Antiquarians' men driven by curiosity, a cross between early archaeologisits and treasure hunters, made the discovery in 1808.

Fortunately for us they kept careful notes and had an illustrator with them when they catalogued the four thousand year-old grave goods. Amongst them they listed a golden chest lozenge decorated with concise lines, a solid gold belt buckle and bronze artefacts including a beautiful axe and the two largest bronze knives ever found in Britain. One of the knives had a hilt decorated with tiny gold pins arranged with stupefying skill into a flashing herringbone pattern. Closer examination of the chest lozenge reveals the sheer brilliance of our ancestors, as the angle at its top is the exact difference between the angles of the setting sun on both the summer and winter solstices. It's precisely eighty-one degrees and those ancient Britons worked that out two thousand years before Pythagorus is supposed to have created the science of geometry. For me they are the sacred angles of Stonehenge.

Fragments of wood and some copper pins, first thought to be the remains of a shield, are I'm assured associated with the knives. However I like the idea proposed by some, that they're actually parts of an alidade or surveying table, which the lozenge could have been laid on to make astronomical sightings. I'd love that to be true and I can't help feeling if they'd made one for the king then put it in his grave, they must have kept a spare of such an important observational instrument. Maybe one with the angles inscribed on cheaper copper rather than expensive gold but I wouldn't mind that at all. I keep hoping there's one lying out there somewhere on Salisbury Plain waiting for me to find it.

What of the grave itself? Well, Bush Barrow is half a mile South-West of Stonehenge as the crow flies. And if the crow flies on the Winter Solstice its course will be unerringly into the sun, which on that day sets directly behind Bush Barrow when viewed from Stonehenge. No other spot in that sacred landscape could have held more honour or ritual significance and in those times the chalk mound of the Barrow would have been carefully tended to remain white so the setting sun would have formed a fantastic halo around the grave.

These days the grave goods are known as the Bush Barrow Collection and for a long time they've been owned by the Wiltshire Heritage Museum, a handsome building with a stone portico, in the market town of Devizes on the edge of Salisbury Plain. Unfortunately for decades the real artefacts were metaphorically reburied in a local bank vault because the museum simply didn't have a gallery secure enough to have them insured for display. Visitors were treated instead to the sight of replicas, which weren't too bad but were hardly the real thing.

I was a regular visitor to the museum around 2009 while researching a novel and I struck up a friendship with the museum's director David Dawson. David's dream was to liberate the real artefacts from their imprisonment in the bank vault so that people could see them and wonder. That would need a lot of money, which the museum simply didn't have. I was thinking a lot about Bush Barrow in those days and I had an idea.

It's fair to say the first time I saw the wonderful artefacts from that spectacular grave I fell under their spell and I'm going to tell you about the sticks, one in particular and hundreds of others too, which are crucial to the Bush Barrow story. And so it's time I introduced you to another item found in the grave; the sceptre. It's an orb of polished stone, which was originally mounted on a stick decorated with collars of bone carved into zigzag flashes. The stone itself is dun coloured, and far less flashy than the gold and bronze but it obviously had powerful significance not only because it was a rare kind of fossil but also because of this stick. Sadly the 'lightning stick' disintegrated almost before the antiquarian's eyes when they exposed it to the air after millennia in the grave but it had obviously served a vital purpose in elevating the polished fossil from a simple orb to a sceptre. It is the first deliberately fashioned symbol of high office known in the British Isles.

And that's where other sticks played their part in the creation of this extraordinary story. You see, in order that the 'lightning stick' could fit the fossil orb had to have a hole drilled through it. No diamond tipped power tools in those days so they used a bow drill, rather like the ones used for starting fires. They would spin a stick around on the bow and string while pouring on sand and a little water as an abrasive to work away at the fossil. It's been estimated it took five hundred or more man-hours to complete that job alone. More proof, surely, that its owner must been a king and given the significance of the grave's location it does not seem too much of a stretch to say he was the King of Stonehenge and so I put my idea to my friend David Dawson.

"David," I asked, "Could you call the Bush Barrow Collection the First Crown Jewels of Britain?"

"Well, you might Alun but then you're a journalist. I wouldn't but then I'm a scientist," he said.

"But in principle?"

"It's true that at the time the antiquarians called them 'Insignia of Dignity' which they certainly are and there's nothing of a similar nature before them so I suppose it wouldn't be wrong to characterise them in that way."

That was all I needed to know as I put in a call to an old friend, Paul Harris, a Daily Mail feature writer. "Paul, how would you like to see the first Crown Jewels of Britain," I asked.

"I'd love to!"

A week later we were in the conference room of the museum as David and an assistant, both white-gloved like magicians, unpacked a plain black box that had been brought from the bank vault. One by one the grave goods were laid out on a velvet cloth and I hope it's not too fanciful to say I could feel the age-old power of those items crackling in the air. Paul too was completely entranced by the collection and had more than enough material for the piece he was going to write. As he was leaving we shook hands and he said, "You and I have seen a lot of things Al, but I've never felt the hairs on the back of my neck go up quite like that before."

It seems that Paul's placing the importance of the Bush Barrow hoard in its true perspective helped swing the grants that would make a new, secure gallery possible. Money was just the start, of it of course. It took four more years of patient commitment and hard work on the part of David Dawson but eventually I was delighted to receive an email thanking me for my small part in it all and inviting me to the grand opening of a new, secure gallery where the Bush Barrow Collection, together with stunning gold finds from other Bronze Age graves in Wiltshire, would be displayed at long last. Anyone with more than a passing interest in Stonehenge, Britain's greatest heritage site, and the nature and sophistication of our Bronze Age ancestors should absolutely take a trip to Devizes to see the original Crown Jewels of Britain and meet the King of Stonehenge. They won't disappoint.

The Bush Barrow Sceptre is just one example of the ancient and widespread use of sticks as symbols of power and authority. It's a simple enough concept, a special kind of stick is invested with power, whether divine or political, which signals the bearer should be treated with a particular respect. Let's fast forward a thousand years from Bush Barrow and travel to the Nile Valley in Ancient Egypt where things were building up to the biggest 'stick off' in history. At least that's what we've been led to believe by the Bible. I'm referring of course to the blockbuster story of the Exodus; a drama that could not have happened without some vital props. That's right, sticks. It doesn't matter whether you think the Bible is the word of the Lord or simply a collection of fantastic myths because in some ways the stories that cultures choose to tell about themselves can reveal as much about them as their archaeology.

At the time the Land of the Pharaohs was awash with sticks, which were used as emblems of office and authority, from the Pharaoh himself who carried wands, albeit made of gold, representing a hook and a flail, down to the wooden sceptres and staffs of court officers and lesser officials of the kingdom. Richly decorated, these sticks represented both earthly and heavenly power. They were the sticks of the gods.

One early sceptre of wood, found in the Valley of the Kings, was carved to resemble a bundle of reeds and high-ranking officials also carried Was Sceptres, which were long staffs with a canine head, usually of bronze, with a forked or pronged end. The list goes on and on. They had Mekes Staffs, Hetes and Heqa Sceptres; Sekhem and Kherep rods too. All were used as various badges of office but also in the conduct of religious offerings and they were in daily use by royalty and high officials in a complex hierarchical system of sacred stick power.

During the reign of Rameses the Old Testament says the Israelites were being held as enforced bricklayers to build a city for the Pharaoh although there is scant archaeological evidence to prove the truth of this. They were enslaved, says the Bible, and living in appalling conditions until Moses came along carrying a simple, undecorated wooden staff in obvious contrast to those of the Egyptians. Most of us know the story. Using this staff as a conduit for the Lord's power Moses brought down terrible plagues on the Egyptians. There were inundations of frogs and snakes, a plague of boils, the Nile flowed with blood and finally every firstborn son of Egypt died on the night of the Passover. Ramses was forced to relent and let the Israelites go. But he changed his mind and pursued the fleeing slaves until Moses used his staff to part the Red Sea allowing his people to reach the far shore and the Promised Land. Moses conveniently closed the waters behind them to drown the Egyptian army.

The Book of Exodus also tells us Moses had a wingman in Aaron, who wielded a power staff too. Aaron cast his down and turned it into a snake at which Pharaoh's sorcerers decided to see him and raise him by turning their sceptres into serpents as well. Proper light sabre stuff until we're told Aaron's snake ended the stand off by simply eating the sorcerers' reptiles. As a story it's pure Monotheistic, one-God propaganda against the Egyptians who worshipped many Gods with a large dash of Ophism or snake worship in their religious calendar. Ophism was a common component of many world religions but not one a jealous, singular God could possibly countenance so naturally Aaron's snake was able to snack on the others. It's absolutely right for me to say that if you take the story literally then it is the foundation of your religious faith and of course I respect that too.

At which point, while we're still in Egypt, I'd like to address the question I posed earlier about dogs, sticks and retrieving. Well, amongst Tutankhamen's many grave goods was a collection of throwing sticks and boomerangs, which were commonly used in Ancient Egypt for wildfowling in the huge papyrus reed beds of the Nile Delta. Significantly throwing sticks will not return to their owner after clobbering a duck. We also know the Egyptians revered hunting dogs and called them Setem. There's no way a human could find a duck that had been struck and fallen amongst the endless acres of reeds but a Setem could. With your supper brought to hand of course you'd send the dog back to retrieve your favourite, hand carved throwing stick rather than lose it. I know about retrievers, I have three working dogs myself and they love fetching things. And I think the reason dogs and sticks go together so happily has its roots in hunting with throwing sticks. I wonder how you say, "Fetch" in Ancient Egyptian.

The Romans had a bit of a Power Stick fetish too. The Civil arm of the Empire had a potent icon that relied on a bundle of sticks. It was called Fasces and it was a cluster of wooden rods tied together to wrap around an axe in its centre, the head of the axe being visible. An official called a Lictor, whose job it was to deliver the punishments meted out by his master, carried the Fasces bundle ahead of a magistrate or consul. The axe in the bundle served as a potent reminder of the possibility of death if you broke the rules in the Roman world. In the 1930's pompous Italian leader Mussolini revived the Fasces as a symbol of Italy's empowerment and that's where we get the word Fascist.

The Roman military icon is of course the Eagle, which was often personally awarded by the Emperor as a Standard to each Legion. The Aquila was a golden representation of Roman might that marched at the head each Legion and was a focus of immense pride among the soldiers. The loss of an Eagle in battle was a source of huge disgrace and the Romans would take extreme measures to find one that had been lost. When, for instance, the German tribes at the Forest of Totenberg annihilated three legions the Empire spent decades trying to recover the Eagles of those legions and four of them were won back. Naturally the Aquila had to be seen by the soldiers of the Legion and for that to happen it needed a stick, a long pole to be exact, and was carried by an ensign called a Signifer who wore a bearskin over his helmet to distinguish him.

Let your mind wander back to AD 60 and we'll tag along behind the Signifer of the XIV Gemina Legion commanded by an utterly ruthless general called Suetonius Paulinus. He had marched, probably from Gloucester, to the shores of Anglesey in North Wales; an island the Romans called Mona Insula, derived from its Celtic name of Mon. Anglesey had been a thorn in the Empire's side since the conquest of Britain. Rebellious tribal folk and hundreds of outlawed Druids, both men and women were allowed to be priests, had fled there and used it as a base to foment more insurrection against the Empire. It's a large island and one of the few, good wheat growing areas in the mountainous geography of Wales.

The Romans particularly loathed the Druids for a number of reasons and one of the main ones was the Celtic belief system called metempsychosis. The Celts believed that when they died their spirits would immediately inhabit another body either in this dimension or another; basically they held a very early belief in quantum being. That philosophy manifested in a quite fearless approach to battle that cost the ruthlessly efficient Romans dear in terms of casualties. It's true the Romans were quite laid back about assimilating the gods and traditions of conquered tribes but only on the Empire's terms. This happened in Britain too in places like Bath where Sula, the local goddess of the famous hot springs, was adopted and the Roman settlement there named Aqua Sulis in her honour.

But there was little slack given to the Druids who were judges and administrators as well as priests in Celtic culture and were obstinate in their opposition to Roman rule. Julius Caesar, the Emperor's Augustus, Claudius and Tiberius all took punitive measures against the Druids. Their sacred groves were destroyed, their practices outlawed and those who carried Druid insignia executed. The tribal structure of the Gauls and their Druid priests were eradicated in a co-ordinated genocide organised by no less a figure than Julius Caesar himself. It's against this background that Suetonius marched on Anglesey.

By far the largest of the Welsh islands it is separated from the mainland by the Menai Straits, which are a narrow funnel for fierce tidal races and quick sands. These were the strategic problems Suetonius had to overcome if he were to triumph. The Roman chronicler Tacitus brings the scene alive in a spine tingling description that I first heard when my son Harry, who studied Classics at Oxford, translated it from the Latin one evening. It was a special moment for me and this is roughly what Harry read out as he translated from the page:

> *Suetonius Paulinus prepared to attack the island of Mona, which had a considerable population of its own, whilst also serving as a haven for refugees. In view of the shallow channel he had a flotilla of boats with flat bottoms constructed. By this method the infantry crossed; the cavalry, who followed, did so by fording or, in deeper water, by swimming at the side of their horses.*

> *On the beach stood their adversaries, a mass of arms and men, with women flitting between the ranks in the style of Furies, in robes of deathly black and with dishevelled hair, brandishing their torches. Together with a circle of Druids, lifting their hands to heaven*

and showering imprecations, they struck the troops with such an awe at the extraordinary spectacle that, as though their limbs were paralysed, they exposed their bodies to wounds without an attempt at movement. Then, reassured by their general, and inciting each other never to cower before a band of females and fanatics, they charged behind the standards, cut down all who met them, and enveloped the enemy in his own flames.

The next step was to install a garrison among the conquered population and to demolish the groves consecrated to their savage cults: for they considered it a pious duty to slake the altars with captive blood and to consult their deities by means of human entrails.

It was then, at the very moment of victory, that a messenger brought Suetonius some extremely bad news indeed. Some of the accounts of what happened were written decades after the events but they're all we have and they ring true and the report must have been shocking even for a seasoned Roman general. It told Suetonius that three hundred miles away on the flat, farmland of East Anglia the use of some different Roman sticks had cost the Empire some eighty thousand lives in what, I believe, is one of the first revolts in recorded history that is feminist in its essential nature.

The Roman Centurion's badge of office and instrument of punishment is a Vine Stick; rather like a modern officer's 'swagger stick.' Stripped, first beaten with a Vine Stick, then flogged and forced to watch her pre-pubescent daughters raped Queen Boudicca of the Iceni became a Fury like her sisters on Anglesey and a feminist Fury at that. Let me explain. Boudicca was wife of Prasutagus the ruler of the Iceni but to those Iron Age warrior people she was also the living embodiment of Adastre, the war goddess. Prasutagus was a client king to the Romans and paid them with military allegiance and taxes in the form of wheat and gold. In those times the long held tradition amongst the Celtic tribes was to afford women more or less equal rights. Women of the tribes had the right to own property, the right to refuse marriage and the right to divorce if they were unhappily married. They could be tribal chieftains or war leaders and many women became Druid priestesses and seers. Definitely not the Roman way, however, as they preferred to treat women as property and afforded them few rights if any at all.

As a client king Prasutagus drew up a Will that shared his huge farming estate between his two daughters and the Emperor, who happened to be that notorious man Nero. This did not go down well with the Romans who saw a share between two females and an Emperor as a vile insult and so when Prasutagus died the Imperial Procurator in Britain, the brutish Declanus Catus went straight to East Anglia and seized the land. And this was when he made a very Roman point by ordering the infamous flogging of Boudicca and the rape of her girls. The Roman whip or flagrum consisted of a short stick with three or four leather thongs attached to it. Sometimes the thongs held small iron balls or pieces of sheep bone, to inflict maximum damage. It was indeed an excruciatingly painful implement. At any rate Boudicca survived the scourge. Most didn't, which makes me wonder whether it might have been more of a symbolic punishment and if that is the case the symbolism wasn't lost on the Iceni people. The Romans had humiliated and shamed their living goddess so up the Iceni rose as one.

The Roman chronicler Dio Cassius leaves us this description of the formidable Queen Goddess of the Iceni:

> *"She was huge of frame, terrifying of aspect, with a harsh voice. A great mass of bright red hair fell to her*

knees. She wore a great twisted golden necklace and a tunic of many colours, over which was a thick mantle, fastened by a brooch. Now she grasped a spear to strike fear into all who watched her..."

The first thing the warrior queen did was to lead the Iceni army of one hundred thousand warriors against the Roman capital of Britain at Camulodunum; modern Colchester. There they butchered the Ninth Legion, sacked the city and set it alight causing a layer of red ash that's still present and called the Boudicca Destruction Horizon by archaeologists. It has a certain ring to it doesn't it? Verulamiam, the city of St. Albans was next and then she moved on with a powerful force of chariots to the booming port of Londinium on the Thames. By the time she'd sacked these three major Roman garrisons the chroniclers of the Empire say that eighty thousand people had been killed. Paradoxically it's also said Boudicca reserved the worst of her feminine spite for captive Roman women and Dio Cassius gives us this awful account of what happened to them in London.

> *"...their breasts were cut off and stuffed in their mouths, so that they seemed to be eating them, then their bodies were skewered lengthwise on sharp stakes"*

Roman propaganda? Perhaps but I don't think so, not this time, after all Boudicca was undoubtedly in a volcanic rage and I believe the symbolism of those barbaric acts is strikingly obvious, well it is to me at least. Boudicca was sending out a message that said, loud and clear, "This is what happens to the breasts that suckle the monsters of Rome." I suspect that in Boudicca's eyes those women weren't members of any sisterhood in a tribal manifestation of sexual equality but women who actively perpetuated Roman inequality. In any event she dealt with them savagely.

While all this butchery was going on Suetonius and his Legion, fresh from their own dismembering of the Druids, was on a forced march south and eventually met the Celtic horde, by then swelled to two hundred thousand warriors, somewhere on the Roman road called Watling Street. It's then that the chronicler Tacitus gifts us with Boudicca's last battle call to her troops the night before they met Suetonius' army. It is, in my view, nothing less than an ancient and stirring manifesto for women's rights and Boudicca's last known words must surely reverberate down the ages as a clarion call to anyone who believes in those rights.

> *"We (the Celts) are used to the leadership of women but I came back before you not as a queen of a distinguished line but as an ordinary woman, my body cut by the lash; avenging the loss of my liberty and the outrages imposed on my daughters. Roman greed spares neither the bodies of the old or virgins. The gods were on our side in our quest for vengeance. One legion has already perished and the others are cowering in their forts to escape. When the Romans realize their small force and the justice of our cause they will know it is victory or death. This is my resolve as a woman. Follow me or submit to the Roman yolk."*

Not until the Spanish Armada was sailing up the Channel to invade England do we hear anything like it again. This time another great British Queen addressed her troops when Elizabeth I, standing at Tilbury docks, urged them to the defence of the nation with these famous words…

> *'I know I have the body but of a weak and feeble woman; but I have the heart and stomach of a king, and a king of England too, and I think foul scorn that Parma or Spain, or any prince of Europe, should dare*

to invade the borders of my realm: to which rather
than any dishonour shall grow by me, I myself will take
up arms, I myself will be your general.'

Brave words indeed, just has Boudicca's words fifteen hundred years earlier had been. However there's less actual substance to the Tudor Queen's words than those of the Iceni monarch's not least because by then Elizabeth was the only woman in the realm who could claim equal rights with men and then only by dint of her Crown.

Elizabeth was never really going to charge into battle, or become their general but Boudicca was always going to be in the thick of the fighting and leading her army.

Still Boudicca's spirit seems to resonate in Elizabeth's words and the more I read those two speeches the more I'm convinced Elizabeth is actually channelling Boudicca in her famous address at Tilbury. You see, as a young princess, Elizabeth had a distinct advantage over most other women of her day because she was given a formal education. By the time she was eleven years old she could speak French, Italian, Spanish, Welsh (the language of her Tudor forebears) and crucially Latin. She was also completely fascinated by the study of history according to her tutors. I for one really can't believe that a Latin-studying, history-loving British princess would not have read the Roman accounts of the invasion of Anglesey and Boudicca's revolt. Perhaps she'd even had to translate them as an exercise for her Latin master. Then, when the Armada crisis was upon her, the tone and timbre of Boudicca's defiant address to her warriors would have come back to mind when Elizabeth most needed to hear and be inspired by them.

The Iceni and their tribal allies did indeed respond to Boudicca's clarion call and followed their flame haired warrior goddess into battle. But this time they suffered a dreadful defeat at the hands of the heavily outnumbered but highly disciplined Romans. This time it was the turn of the Iceni to suffer and more than eighty thousand Celts were put to the sword. And if you don't accept this was an essentially feminist uprising against the Romans then I should tell you that no less a figure than the Roman general Suetonius himself reported there were more women than male warriors in Boudicca's host and urged his soldiers into battle saying:

> *"There are more women than men in their ranks. They are not soldiers, they're not even properly equipped."*

No one really knows what happened to Boudicca. Some say she took poison, others that she fell ill and died but we do know her body was never found although there's speculation she's buried at the Birdlip escarpment overlooking Gloucester. I like to dream she slipped North of the Wall to the wild Celtic lands of Scotland and saw her days out with her daughters. And oh, how different it might all have been but for the use of Roman sticks on a living goddess.

In the days of Elizabeth I, Good Queen Bess as she was known, key officers of state at the Tudor court were entitled to carry symbolic staffs of office too. Most of these honorifics are no longer in use with one notable exception and that's Black Rod, the Sergeant at Arms of the House of Lords. He uses his Rod to summon the Members of Parliament from the Commons to hear the Queen's Speech in the Lords by bashing it on the door of the Chamber. Back in the days of Elizabeth the two most feared men in the Kingdom both carried staffs of office and they didn't do so to employ them in Parliamentary theatrics. Their staffs were indicators of real power.

One of those men was William Cecil, the Queen's Principal Secretary, an early sort of Prime Minister, who regularly carried a long, shoulder length white staff. The other was

Elizabeth's formidable spymaster Francis Walsingham, the scourge of Catholic plots against the Crown. As Lord Privy Seal and Chancellor of the Duchy of Lancaster he was entitled to carry two staffs of office if he wanted. Chillingly both these men had access to the keys of the Tower of London and its infamous torture chamber but they used their power successfully to defend their Queen and the Protestant ascendancy in England.

Centuries later in the United States of America in 1856 another stick was used to brutally reinforce a point when Senator Charles Sumner made an anti-slavery speech against politicians from the Southern States, particularly Carolina, whom he accused of being complicit in the evil. Inevitably the arguments on both sides were incendiary and pretty vile with the slavery lobby accusing abolitionists of simply wanting to get rid of the practice so they could have sex with black women. In turn abolitionists pointed with much justification to the enforced sexual domination and rape of black women by slave owners. A more unseemly, appalling debate is hard to imagine these days.

The situation was a powder keg and it exploded two days after Sumner's speech when Linton Brooks, a Democratic Senator from South Carolina, and a slave owner to boot, walked into the Senate, carrying a walking cane with a gold knob, and proceeded to viciously and relentlessly beat Sumner. Sumner tried to escape by crawling under a desk but Brooks kept on beating him and did so until the cane broke. It was a savage and sustained attack, which saw Sumner unable to return to political duties for three years. Brooks was hailed a hero in the Southern States for defending their honour and that adulation in the South was heightened when he was fined a paltry $300 for the assault but avoided imprisonment.

The characters in that drama played out on the floor of America's legislative chamber didn't know it then but they were simply rehearsing the enormous splits developing in American society. Five years later those profound schisms would see the States plunged into a dreadful Civil War. One hundred and forty thousand, four hundred and fourteen men would die before it ended. If only Americans could have read the signs they'd have realised Brooks' gold-topped cane was a finger-post pointing ominously in the direction of disaster and maybe, just maybe, they might have taken another path and abolished slavery without going to war. If only they had.

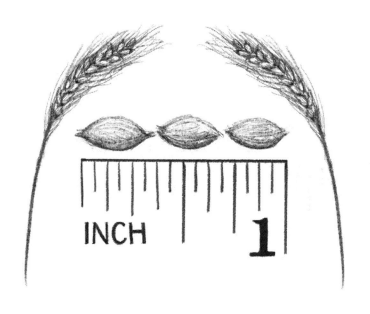

Chapter 3
STICKS RULE

Every year the British Army celebrates the Queen's Birthday with a piece of military theatre on a parade ground known as 'Horseguards' at the end of the Mall in London. It is meticulously staged, and I use the word advisedly, with hundreds of the Queen's red-coated, bearskin-hatted Guards at their ceremonial best. It's called the Trooping of the Colour and, while the top brass of the Brigade of Guards orchestrate the whole thing, the precision drill is controlled by a few very special sticks in the hands of a breed of sticklers called Colour Sergeants. They ensure that when those ultra smart Guardsmen step onto Horseguards Parade they do so with metronomic precision because they have been drilled and schooled with an instrument of parade ground torture called a Pace Stick.

Pace Sticks look like a giant set of geometry compasses, which many will remember more fondly from school than I do. In the case of the Guards regiments they are beautiful rosewood sticks with brass headpieces and ferrules all polished to infallibility. The British army actually has a School of Ceremonial based in Catterick, Yorkshire where the secret ways of the Pace Stick are taught on formal courses and there's even a World Pace Sticking Championship with most contenders coming from the British-trained armies of the former colonies of the Commonwealth. Attention! In case it should ever come up as a question in a pub quiz the regulation pace for quick and slow marches is thirty inches. So, with a ceremonial flourish the Brigade of Guards' fixation with the precise measurement of a soldier's step neatly illustrates man's obsession with accurate measurement.

It's hard to say when mankind first felt this urge to measure things but I can imagine the motive was for sharing. Picture a group of hunters returning to camp to give the clan matriarch news of a kill that needed to be processed. The whole community would have to turn out to paunch, skin and butcher the life-sustaining quarry and I imagine the conversation would go something like this…

"We've killed a mammoth."

"Brilliant! How big is it?"

"About six spears long and four at the shoulder."

"Blimey, that's a big one. That'll be enough to keep us going through the winter. And it's time I got a new bed spread too, this one's wearing thin."

Told the kill was six spears by four the matriarch would have been able to picture what the villagers had to deal with straight away. It's fair to assume that clans in certain geographical locations with specific quarry species would have routinely produced and used spears of a certain type and length giving a nod to the standard length that would come millennia later. And that's probably how it went on for thousands of years. Every land mass and every region of that land would have used sticks of a roughly standard length as a crude but reasonably effective unit of measurement. The methods used by our ancient forebears are a far cry from the laser and digital micro electronic instruments we employ in the 21st Century but the spear, and later the measuring stick, served their purpose in their time; and that was a very long time indeed.

In fact I still use my own stick for 'rule of thumb' measurements when I'm in the countryside. I know it's just a fraction over three feet long from its tip to the bottom of the V-shape that forms the thumb grip; a yardstick in fact. Would a gap be wide enough to get a vehicle through? My stick will tell me. I also use it as a rough and ready depth gauge. You won't catch me crossing some particularly wet, boggy ground without testing ahead with my stick. The same goes for streams with muddy bottoms. The depth of water might not go over the top of my wellington boots but if the mud below is two feet deep that would be a different and far wetter outcome indeed without my stick.

However the measurement of weight in the dawn of humanity's time was a different kettle of fish to that of the measurement of length. Let's imagine the conversation when the joints and cuts of mammoth meat were being shared out amongst members of the clan. It's reasonable to assume the chieftain or the matriarch would oversee the division of meat and that would happen after the hunters, those who'd taken part in the actual kill, had taken their share. When that was done great lumps of meat would be severed from the carcass and handed over to each of the clan members.

"Here's your share," the senior woman would say as she handed a joint of flesh to someone.

"Hang on, hang on," he might have moaned, nodding in the direction of a woman nearby, "She's had a lot more meat than me."

The matriarch would eye him up and down then take both joints to test them against each other, one in each hand, as she scaled their weight simply by the feel. Depending on the status or popularity of the complainant she might say, "Yeah, you're right, here's a bit more." Or she might decide, "Nah, they're about the same. Like it or lump it."

This state of affairs must have lasted for a very, very long time until someone, somewhere hit on the idea of balancing items on scales to give a true and fair comparison of weights. As you might know to make a pair of scales you would first need two plates of the same weight but most importantly a stick to hang them off and act as a see-saw balance. As far as I know the first known set of scales of this style was found in the Valley of the River Indus, in present-day Pakistan, and was dated to around 2000 BC.

Such simple scales, with a stick as a balance, gave way to more sophisticated mechanisms with the demands of increasing trade between growing city-based economies. Some were developed from a combination of metal and wood, others were all metal. That they were very important is not in doubt and the Ancient Egyptians portrayed Anubis, their God of Embalming, as half man half dog, weighing the hearts of the dead to decide who should be allowed to enter the heavenly underworld. It wasn't until the 18th Century, and then in order to meet the pressing needs of an increasingly industrial society, that weighing technology moved on from this basic model of the balance scales.

Although they were surprisingly accurate in the hands of an honest broker, balance scales were notoriously easy to manipulate and cheat, which was yet another reason why the Romans loathed the Celts and eventually set out to subjugate them all; more of that concept later. It's not commonly known but in 390 BC, when Rome was still a developing entity, a large army of Celtic tribes, under a paramount chief called Brennus, swept down from the hills of Northern Italy and Austria to invade and capture the city.

The Celts were never ones for hanging about for too long and Rome wasn't to their taste not least because it was surrounded by a nasty, mosquito-infested swamp so they decided to return to their own hearths set in the fragrant air of the Alpine valleys. But they certainly weren't going to go home empty handed and Brennus demanded one thousand pounds in gold from the thoroughly beaten-up Romans. They agreed and Brennus proceeded to weigh it on his own, rigged scales. When the Romans complained about this obvious cheating Brennus simply laid his sword onto his side of the scales, demanded yet more gold to match it, and summed it all up for the furious Romans with a simple truth. "Woe to the vanquished," Brennus bluntly told them. The Romans never forgot Brennus and ever after bore a grudge against the Celts.

As I say weight measurement didn't develop very much at all until modern times but the measurement of distance did, propelled by the emergence of agriculture and then by the needs of the architects and surveyors who created the world's first great cities and temples. It was, pardon the pun, imperative to them that they had an accurate and, more importantly, standard unit of measurement. Obviously different cultures developed different standard units of length and there's a bewildering list of cubits, feet, hands, poles, chains, furlongs and many, many more around the world. We had to wait a long while for global standards to be established.

Another conversation imagined, this one between some farmers in an emerging agricultural community. Let's say it's the late Neolithic and there's a dispute over how they'll share out the work to cultivate grain on the most fertile land in their area.

"I know what we should do," says one farmer, "We'll share out the land in strips and each strip will be the width of seven lengths of our staves laid in a line."

"That's not a bad idea," says another, "The only trouble is your staff is at least two hands longer than mine because you're taller."

"Two hands is nothing," says the first farmer.

"You say that but it's an extra half a staff's length on your strip when you add it up."

A third farmer pipes up, "Let's ask the Chief if we can use his staff to measure all the strips. That way we all get the same size to work. That's fair." They agree and the Chief's stave becomes the unit of measurement in that one, tiny corner of the planet. The fact it's his staff being used for such an important task also underpins the Chief's status endowing him with much Stick Power. Everyone is happy and we have the start of metrology, which is the science of measurement and not to be confused with predicting the weather. It may also tell us the way the practical roots of simple mathematics began.

Once they'd got the idea our ancestors were relatively quick to develop the art and science of measurement to help them achieve their fantastically grand visions for buildings that still fill us with wonder. This happened in different cultures at different times and I suppose the architecture of the Egyptians, which began to manifest itself five thousand years ago, is a good benchmark of the techniques involved.

Surveying in Egypt had its roots in the annual flooding of large swathes of productive farmland in the Nile Delta. Each year the property rights of hundreds of farmers, whose land had been inundated and partly washed away, had to be re-established to head-off heated disputes and unrest in the population.

Sticks were vital to the endeavour and to the grand designs that followed; four types in particular. Wooden stakes, knocked into the ground in their thousands, were just one of the stick types they needed. There were three others, which were more sophisticated and used as line of sight instruments for surveying. Of these one was called a 'merchet', a long, straight staff, with a slit cut into its top to allow light through and give the surveyor line of sight onto other upright poles called gnomon used to create shadows from the sun to establish the orientation of buildings. The merchet was also used to take sights off ropes and plumb lines; lead weights suspended on a string to give a true vertical. The other surveying instrument was called a 'groma,' which was basically a right angle, set square type of instrument that could also carry a plumb line. With these simple instruments the Egyptian master builders were able to lay out the Pharaohs' cities and their gigantic tombs simply by marking out the stakes then joining them with special measuring ropes, which were treated with resin and beeswax to prevent shrinkage and to hold their length. Let's face it. No sticks, no Pyramids.

Most of what we know about Egyptian techniques comes from hieroglyphics and from tomb paintings; two in particular show famous surveyors at work. One is a man called Djeserkeresonb and he's depicted recording the measurements as 'rope stretchers' are seen in the background. The other is the tomb of Menna, who is seen carrying his 'merchet', his surveying pole, while nearby is a coiled-up measuring rope. These are expensive burials showing the high status of these specialist surveyors and the crucial nature of their work for Egyptian society.

There had been complex architectural cultures before the Egyptians and they weren't the only sophisticated society on the planet to perfect methods of surveying. With some variations different cultures around the globe discovered and used the same sort of surveying techniques to construct dramatic and wonderful buildings of brick or stone or both. The Sumerians, Assyrians, Greeks, Romans, Persians, the Ancient Hindus, the Chinese, the Aztecs, Mayans and Ancient African cultures all used variations of much the same techniques. This type of surveying, using poles, stakes, plumb lines, shadows and string, continued down the ages right into the Medieval period.

A time travelling Egyptian 'harpendonaptae', as they called their surveyors, would not have been at all fazed by the methods employed by the masons constructing Salisbury

Cathedral in the 12th Century. It has to be said the building and surveying approach of one 13th Century South American culture is more of a mystery and just how the Inca people of Peru and Bolivia constructed their huge, complex and almost entirely earthquake proof walls is still a matter of conjecture. There are many theories but I'll eat my hat if sticks weren't involved.

Of course, it's all very well having surveying instruments but they're absolutely no use whatsoever without a standard measurement of length. Most cultures hit on the idea of a cubit, which is the length of a man's arm from elbow to fingertip. Interestingly different societies had different cubit lengths demonstrating that, thankfully, we're not all the same. The foot is another one of course, the Roman foot being a bit small compared to others, and then there's the hand, which was generally the width of four fingers and is still used to this day for measuring the height of horses up to the shoulder.

Once again taking the Egyptians as an example we can see they had a complicated but efficient measuring scale that allowed them to construct huge buildings that are wonders of geometry. Sad to say I suffer from chronic innumeracy but basically multiplication and division in Egyptian mathematics was done by only having to multiply two and ten so that all smaller numbers were factors of those two numbers. Egyptian surveyors used a Royal Cubit, which I assume was the measurement of an early Pharaohs limb. They applied this to a rope, not unlike the surveyors' chain used until quite recently in our own society, to get the standard building measurement, which was one hundred Royal Cubits long.

Simple. Take some ropes of uniform lengths, a few vertical poles, a plumb line, quite a lot of sticks, loads of big stone blocks and there you go; you've got your Pyramid.

My friend Matt Richards is a Wiltshire based builder and a practical sort of man. He reckons that if push came to shove he could build a pyramid. As with all builder's estimates there are some provisos. It wouldn't be cheap. Of course not Matt. There might be a few 'extras' or unforeseen costs. Goes without saying mate. And he'd have to have some heavy plant for the excavating and lifting. It would be do-able but not without some pegs and string, maybe a modern aerosol marker, to plan out the ground.

"It might be a bit of a wobbly pyramid but it would be a pyramid," said Matt, "Bricklayers still use string and pegs to get their levels. I use them if I have to lay concrete and the truth is no-one's come up with a more practical way of dong small construction jobs like that."

He's right, of course, and they've had four or five thousand years to find something better. As I mentioned Matt lives in Wiltshire where some other world-renowned architects and surveyors once lived. They're the folk who built Stonehenge and the Bush Barrow giant must surely have been one of them. You remember his golden chest lozenge contained the precise angle of difference between sunsets at the two Solstices. Pretty remarkable and just in case there's any doubt no less a body than the Royal Astronomical Society concluded nearly a decade ago that the great Trilithon Stones of the Henge were deliberately aligned to predict and observe the Solstice sun.

These same experts also believe Stonehenge was deliberately laid out to track the passage of the moon especially when the tilt of the earth puts the moon's passage on its extreme northern and southern paths; a phenomenon described as a 'major standstill.' Because of these observations the Royal Society has been moved to the foundation of a relatively new branch of science called archaeoastronomy supervised by a very active Astronomical Heritage Committee. Exciting stuff when you realize there are over two thousand Stone monuments, in various states of dilapidation across the islands of Britain and probably many more that have vanished over time. In the Aberdeen area of Scotland, and the Cork and Kerry areas in Ireland, there are some fascinating monuments called Recumbent Stone Circles. There are about two hundred in total and they most often feature a large stone or monolith lying on its side absolutely aligned to the passage of the moon in its southern arc.

No one truly knows what these monuments were for but it's safe to assume there was a strong element of moon worship attached to their construction. My partner Stephanie has her own theory though and believes that most of the two and a half thousand known surviving stone circles in the Islands of Britain are aligned to read the passage of the moon. Why? Because even the most technologically savvy, modern chemical-input farmer knows it's best to plant seeds during the new moon. She suspects the farmers of the Neolithic and the Bronze Age were early adherents of biodynamic agriculture, which is predicated on a detailed knowledge of the passage of the moon. That's certainly true of one of the oldest and most remarkable Neolithic monuments in the British Isles…the Stones of Calanais (pronounced Calanish). They stand on the Isle of Lewis, one of the islands of the Outer Hebrides off Scotland's wildly romantic west coast. The Henge is cross-shaped with a central cluster of thirteen giant stones around a small tomb and one of the arms of the cross forms an avenue of nineteen stones to the North East.

Calanais is indescribably beautiful but here's the wonderful thing. It's positioned so that every time the moon is in the south and has a 'major standstill' event in its passage it appears to roll slowly along the hills of the neighbouring island of Great Benera. It then sets by appearing to drop into the centre of the Stone Circle just like a snooker ball falling into a pocket. Amazing! Of course it is but it becomes even more mind boggling when you realize this event only happens once every 18. 6 years; that's roughly five times a century.

How then did they hit upon this awe inspiring Neolithic magic trick, fully five hundred years before the Pyramids were built? Well, I imagine a couple of members of the local clan of farmers and sea harvesters, early crofters if you like, were standing on the spit of land that winds its way to the north east, watching the passage of the moon one 'major standstill' night. The conversation between Hamish and Dougal, let's call them that in honour of our Scots cousins, might have gone something like this…

"Did you see that Dougal?"

"See what?'

"The way the moon fell off the hills and disappeared?"

"I did. I saw that Hamish and my grandmother Flora told me she'd seen it happen years ago too.''

"If that's so it will probably happen again Dougal. Wouldn't it be a grand idea to build a temple here in honour of the moon to mark its passing. Something in stone would look really good. We might even be able to work out when the sun gives us the longest and shortest days too. What d'y say? Shall we give it a go?'

"Well why not? We'll have to ask the others to help but why not?"

"Let's start by planting this staff of mine in the ground here Dougal to mark the point where we saw it happening. Then we can walk in a straight line to mark the spot where we saw the moon fall. Let's do it now before we forget where it happened."

"Good, then we can mark those spots with some rocks and take our staffs back," said Hamish, "Next time we'll bring lots of rods and some line to mark out the places where we can put up some stones but we can start quarrying what we'll need straight away."

Eighteen point six years passed by while Hamish and Dougal watched every moon, waiting to see one roll across the hills and drop into the pocket again. It hadn't happened yet but they were filled with anticipation. Tonight's the night they thought. And it would have been if dark clouds hadn't rushed in heralding lashing rain and a storm that completely obscured the sky. Still the clan didn't forget. Over the next eighteen point six years Hamish drowned while out fishing and Dougal succumbed to old age. But the clan didn't forget. Sitting by the flames of the winter hearth or on long summer days in the heather overlooking the loch, the two of them had shared their vision with their children and grandchildren and the extended family of the tribe had caught the fire of their idea.

Multiples of eighteen point six years came and went and they gathered at Hamish's Stick, as they called the place, to await the rolling moon. Sometimes, to their wonder, the clan watched as it was revealed, at other times it was hidden by fickle clouds. But they knew this was the place and whenever they could they measured and plotted their Stone Circle, and its attendant avenues, with poles and string; all the while hewing stone monoliths from a quarry nearby.

And then around 2900 BC their dreams came to pass and they finally gathered enough measurements to build their stone temple come lunar snooker table. A fanciful account maybe but Calanais is so wonderful that nearly three thousand years later the Ancient Greeks had heard of it by legend and reputation. In the First Century BC the historian, Diodorus, wrote of *"a northern island with a spherical temple dedicated to the moon, who returned every nineteen years and skimmed the earth at a very low height."*

When you look at the Stone constructions of the Ancient Britons and the complex beauty of their gold and bronze artefacts, there's no denying they were a sophisticated people with mathematical knowledge and an intimate association with the heavenly bodies of our solar system. There's also little doubt that the complicated, geometric constructions of their Henge monuments could only have been achieved by using straight sticks and string to lay out their eventual shape and orientation on the ground.

There are nearly as many theories about their methods as there are Stone Circles and one, proposed by Alexander Thom, came up with the notion of a 'Megalithic Yard.' Thom did so after painstakingly measuring and plotting the layout of six hundred sites in England, Scotland, Wales and Brittany. According to Thom the unit by which they were built could only have been 2.72 feet and there was also a Megalithic Rod of two and a half metres. Critics have dismissed the years of work Thom put into this theory out of hand by simply pointing out that his Megalithic Yard is basically the average length of a human pace. Oh dear, I'm the least well equipped person I know to challenge this or any other mathematics based theorem but I do know that Thom's Megalithic Yard is amongst the sanest and least eccentric, not to say crazy, units of measurement used by the inhabitants of the British Isles as we're about to discover.

So let's leave the wonderful history of ancient rulers, by which I mean sticks not kings, behind us while we trace the weird and wonderful evolution of measurement in the British Isles where they went to some pretty strange lengths to find a standard.

I hope my friends in the United States and Canada, and my American partner Dr Stephanie Shelburne of course, will bear with me because the English standard is the one that arrived on the shores of North America with the Founding Mothers and Fathers. With a couple of adjustments that system is still in use in the USA while at home in Britain we abandoned it to fall in line with the European Union and the metric system founded by Napoleon. Roundly defeated by the British at the Battle of Waterloo the Emperor Boney must be laughing his socks off in the grave, while he metaphorically beats us with a metric measuring stick.

At any rate the Romans left our islands in 425AD and the chaos of the Dark Ages followed when the Anglo Saxon invasion and inundation of the British islands began. This was the era of King Arthur (absolutely a real person in my view) and endless conflict with the Saxons who eventually pushed the Celts off the best farmland into the mountains of Wales and Scotland; the far-flung coast of Cornwall too. Few records were kept in those times so we have little idea how things were measured.

Then in the 10th Century we're told the Saxon King Edgar kept a 'yardstick' at his capital in Winchester as the official standard measurement of length. The Saxons also had a longer measurement called the rod; used to work out the acreage of land. Their method of computing the rod was eccentric to say the least. The rod, they said, was the total length of the left feet of the first sixteen men to leave church on Sunday. That's to say any church in the land on any given Sunday. Hardly a universal standard measurement!

Along came the Normans and in time Henry I, who ascended the throne in the year 1100 AD, decreed the 'yard' should be the distance from the tip of his nose to the end of his outstretched thumb; a good bit longer than the old cubit. Nearly one hundred years later in 1196 Richard the Lionheart convened the Assize of Measures where his commissioners transferred the standard yard from a stick to a length of iron or ulna. The Magna Carta confirmed this 'ulna' standardization nineteen years later in the reign of the deeply unpopular King John. Later still, during the thirty-five year reign of Edward I who came to the throne in 1272, the division of the yard into inches and feet was laid down in law. The method of division ordered by the King, who was a couple of yards plus tall and hence known as Longshanks, was quirky to say the least and, believe it or not, revolved around barleycorn. This was what he ruled…

> *'The Iron Ulna of our Lord the King contains three feet and no more; and the foot must contain twelve inches, that is to say, one thirty-sixth part of the said ulna makes one inch, neither more nor less... It is ordained that three grains of barley, dry and round make an inch, twelve inches make a foot; three feet make an ulna; five and a half ulna makes a rod.'*

Where did that idea come from? Who in their right mind could suggest that laying three grains of barley end to end to get an inch would be a good idea? Indeed what was Longshanks on? Be that as it may my partner Stephanie worked out that she stands two hundred and nine barley grains tall in her stocking feet. Go figure, as she would say, in her measured American way.

Various monarchs, including Henry VII, his granddaughter Queen Elizabeth I and George IV, son of George III, who so aggravated the American colonies they kicked him out, dabbled with introducing new, improved yards but essentially the one that Henry VII had ordained in 1492 lasted down the ages and was held, in some reverence, in Parliament together with the standard example of a pound in weight. It's ironic then that a pile of sticks should have put paid to both these ancient standards in1834. They did so in a manner entirely in keeping with the general eccentricity of the evolution of British weights and measures.

I'll explain. Records of deals and contracts struck with government departments were kept on wooden tally sticks, which were usually made of willow and split in two. On one side details of the government's obligations were carved onto the stick; on the other those of the contractor. The Exchequer held the tally sticks as records and the famous diarist Samuel Pepys, who was Clerk to the Navy, would have been entirely familiar with the system. And what a system it was, especially for the officials and contractors who routinely used it to fiddle cash from the Treasury. It was a closed shop system allowing inefficient and corrupt officials to hold onto office and profit from their positions of power by a system of 'sinecures'.

By 1872 the tally stick system had finally reached such a point of disrepute and derision that it was abolished. You might think that would be the end of it but no, too many civil servants in high office had too much at stake and they had clauses put into the Bill keeping their sinecures alive until they had all died. This kept the broken old horse pulling for another fifty-four years until the last of its beneficiaries kicked the bucket. Even then the British government failed to move into the era of paper until 1834; another eight years. What then to do with the thousands of tallies still held by the Treasury?

They decided to burn them and Richard Weobley, the Clerk of Works, was ordered to dispose of them while Parliament was in recess for the autumn. He could have let his workforce take a share home to use as kindling and firewood. Humbug! Tight fisted Richard decided to burn them in the two heating furnaces of the House of Lords, directly below the Chamber.

There were a couple of heavily stacked cartloads to get rid of and they threw the tallies onto a furnace designed for coal, which burns with far less flame than dry wood. The outcome wasn't good. The tally sticks, soaked in a notional tar of greed and cheating, sent their flames roaring up the chimneys, which caught light and sent a fireball blasting through the Chamber of the House of Lords. Parliament with it's wood panelled corridors and offices went up like a torch and with it Henry VII's pound of lead, which melted and ran away. Next to it was Henry's venerable iron yardstick, which succumbed to the flames too. In 1855 a new standard yard was instituted and that stood until the UK went metric in 1965.

Not every billowing cloud of acrid smoke from a fire has a silver lining but this one did, especially as no one was injured in the blaze. The entire Parliament building was destroyed and the government had to commission a new building for the Houses of Parliament. Architect Augustus Pugin was chosen for the new design and came up with a neo-gothic style with a giant three hundred and fifteen feet high clock tower at one end. It had four clock faces and five bells which toll the time every quarter of an hour and on the hour. It's largest bell weighs thirteen and a half tonnes and it's famously called Big Ben. So you see without the intervention of two cart loads of sticks the United Kingdom would be without the clock tower that is the cultural icon by which we are known all over the world. Thank heavens for the sticks that gave us the bell that chimed out our freedom right through the Nazi blitz. No sticks. No Big Ben.

Sticks gave us the first 'rules' imposed on society, which were the standard tabulation of weights and measures that took precedence across the entire country. Later the word came to cover the many aspects of life where a standard set of behaviour was expected. I remember the first ruler I was given. It was a wooden one, a foot long, with the inches and fractions of inches marked along its length. I used it for my first, rudimentary geometry lessons in junior school. I wasn't very good and I clearly remember the use my teacher, Mr Roberts, put my ruler too when confronted with the handiwork of a pupil he recognised as profoundly innumerate. After viewing my pathetic efforts he would pick-up my own ruler to rap me across the knuckles with it. Ouch! I'm afraid it was the first of a small forest of sticks and canes used on me during my schooling at a time when corporal punishment was still legal and much in use in British classrooms and I was very unruly.

So much for school beatings but here's a stick story involving measurement so inspiring, so absolutely off the scale that, once heard, it's impossible to forget. It's also given us a word for a wise man or expert. It's the story of the Pundits and it began in the 1830's when a Welsh geographer was appointed Surveyor General of India. His name was Sir George Everest and there are absolutely no prizes for guessing which mountain was named after him. We know a bit about surveyors already from their ancient predecessors and the principle is the same in the days of the British Raj. Surveyors have to give an accurate measurement of distance and calculate angles to give them height. What goes for a Pyramid goes for a mountain too even if the instruments were more sophisticated in the 19th Century.

Sir George worked on the Great Trigonometric Survey, the GTS as it's known in India, which established the meridian arc from Southern India to Nepal. This was an immense measurement of just under fifteen hundred miles and allowed the accurate mapping of the entire sub-continent. Everest never saw Everest but it was named in his honour in 1852 when his successors managed to survey it and establish it as the world's highest peak. With India mapped there was a more pressing, strategic need for surveying the area known the Roof of the World; the Himalayas, the Karakoram and the Hindu Kush. This vast area comprising Tibet, Nepal, Kashmir as well as territories such Afghanistan and Waziristan was ruled by feudal dynasties and, in Western terms, was ungovernable. But it was an area vital to British interests and Russian ones too as both their Empires washed up to its slopes from India on the British side and the vast Mongolian plains on the Russian.

The British Empire including India, the Jewel in the Crown, had been won across the oceans by a super power Royal Navy. Imperial Russia had a surge in conquests during the Age of Railways, always laying railway track behind them, to establish a hold as they pushed forward. Two strategic lines were actually built by the Russian Army and one of them, the Trans-Caspian Railway, began at Krasnovodsk on the Caspian Sea and ended at Bukhara right on the doorstep of the Roof of the World. Warships on one side; armoured trains the other. The stage was set for a secret war of spies; the classic espionage clash they called The Great Game.

Both sides sent parties of daring young officers into these peculiarly dangerous 'forbidden' regions to scope out the territory. The Russians called their groups of spies 'scientific explorers' the British agents were thinly disguised as 'hunting parties.' But the real harvesting of data was done by a group of twenty astonishingly courageous native Indians called The Pundits who accurately mapped thousands of square miles of hitherto unknown territory. And, as any soldier will tell you, accurate maps are military gold dust. A British officer, Captain T. G. Montgomerie, came up with the idea of the Pundits and his thinking behind the formation of this secret corps of mapmakers was simple. Europeans would make obvious and easy targets for bandits or local rulers looking for a ransom. Natives of the sub-continent however could easily blend into the background especially when disguised as religious pilgrims. And the key to passing themselves off in this way was, of course, that iconic piece of pilgrims' kit, the staff. The

Pundits however carried a staff with a difference, as you're about to discover.

Montgomerie's recruits were put through an exhaustive two-year training in covert map-making at the British Raj's spy school at Dehra Dun. They learnt all the usual espionage skills like learning a convincing cover story, disguises, navigation by the stars and how to escape or evade capture. But then they learnt the extraordinary skills of undercover cartography first developing a uniform pace so that they walked two thousand steps to the mile and counted them off as they did so. This gruelling process involved our old friend sergeant major's pace stick; an instrument of military parade ground bull we've already met. Once this uniform pace had been drummed into them they were taught surveying techniques then provided with a spy kit that James Bond's Q department would be proud to have invented. It included a thermometer and a compass that could be hidden in the top of their pilgrim's staff. The compass is a pretty obvious instrument for a surveyor but the thermometer was used to measure an accurate height in mountainous areas because water boils at different temperatures at different altitudes.

The Pundits also carried specially adapted prayer beads with one hundred beads instead of the traditional one hundred and eight found on Buddhist prayer strings and this they used, together with the standard pace, to measure accurately. The Pundits were also provided with prayer wheels, a common item among pilgrims in the high country close to Tibet. However the prayer wheel was used to record the harvested data carefully written on the paper inside where the prayers should have been. Together with theodolites hidden in false compartments and liquid mercury, carried in a cowrie shell to give them a level for surveying work their kit was complete.

The Pundit's first mission was to accurately map the route from Dehra in India to Kathmandu in Nepal then on to Lhasa, the Forbidden City and capital of Tibet in an eighteen-month odyssey. The two Indians who carried out this amazing feat were Nain Singh, aged thirty-one and his cousin Mani Singh. Nain's code name was The Pundit No.1 and his cousin was referred to in secret despatches as The Patwar. Over the next thirty years the stoic band of just twenty pundits mapped and surveyed a truly enormous geographical area for their British spymasters and, in truth, were amongst the greatest of the Victorian heroes. This was reflected in Kipling's masterpiece Kim which sees the eponymous hero of the thriller, a thirteen year old Anglo Indian boy, taking part in spying missions linked to the Great Game. It's said the famous head of the American CIA, Allen Dulles, kept a copy by his bedside for inspiration.

However the rewards and plaudits accorded by the Establishment to the native Pundits were relatively inappreciable as, of course, in their time they were considered to be inferiors in British colonial culture. The English officers who actually worked with them knew better and revered the Pundits and their achievements. But at the end of the day Montgomerie was awarded the Gold Medal of the Royal Geographical Society while The Pundit No.1 basically got a pat on the back. What a shame, what a terrible shame. I hope and trust that these days those extraordinary men would be showered with honours and medals for their indomitable adventures. I admire them so much I thought I'd honour them in the only way I can by naming them here, with their code names too, and urging you all to read more about them. Peter Hopkirk's wonderful accounts in his books The Great Game and Trespassers on the Roof of the World are a fantastic starting point.

Abdul Hameed...   Mahomed-I-Hameed

Kishen Singh...	A-K, Krishna
Nain Singh…	The Pundit, No 1
Sukh Darshan Singh...	G.S.S.
Mani Singh	G.M., The Patwar
Lama Serap …	Gyatso
Mirza Shuja …	The Mirza
Lala	
Hyder Shah…	The Havildar
Nem Singh…	G.M.N.
Ata Mahomed…	The Mullah
Kinthup…	K.P.
Kalian Singh…	G.K.
Rinzin Namgyal…	R.N.
Hari Ram…	M.H. or No 9
Lama Ugyen Gyatso…	U.G.
Ata Ram Sarat Chandra Das…	S.C.D.
Mukhtar Shah…	M.S.
Alaga	
Abdul Subhan…	A-S

These were great men walking with extraordinary staffs achieving an unbelievable catalogue of missions and accomplishing the seemingly impossible.

*****

Chapter 4
SINISTER STICKS

For millennia sticks in the form of staffs, rods and batons have been used to advertise their owners' devotion to a God or Gods as we've already heard. To be honest this can often be a grey area, as in the case of the Pharaohs who carried an ornate version of a Shepherd's Crook to denote their status. However, as they were technically living gods themselves it could be argued that these Sceptres were more egotistical than devotional objects. No doubt the rods of Moses and Aaron were devotional objects as well as being proto-light sabres; a notion embodied in the line from the famous Psalm 23: "Thy rod and thy staff, they comfort me," although they certainly didn't comfort Pharaoh when the Israelite leaders set them on 'plague' and turned them onto him.

Sticks quickly became glorified and used to signify high rank and power and I believe that stems from the fact that we had needed them to protect, feed and keep us warm from time immemorial. For most of the past five thousand years power in the political sense has been firmly anchored in religion. Top-flight administrators in Rome had the lituus, the ancient staff carried by their augurs. Then Rome began its decline, which I would argue was actually a metamorphosis from a military Empire to a spiritual one embodied in the Roman Catholic Church, and a particular type of stick began to take precedence in the Christian world. This stick goes back to the Hebrew society described in the Old Testament, a pastoral one with entire communities reliant on flocks of sheep and goats, so it's not surprising there are many references to shepherds in the Bible. In their time, the disciples of Jesus of Nazareth came to preach their master was 'the Good Shepherd' and the 'Lamb of God.' They obviously liked these analogies a lot and they stuck so that to this day priests, vicars and pastors refer to their congregations as their 'flock.' Indeed the word 'pastor' comes from the Latin for shepherd. It follows then that the humble shepherds crook evolved, quite rapidly, into one of the great iconic symbols of Christian authority…the Crosier or Bishops Crook.

At first these were simple representations of the wooden implement used by pastoralists to catch a sheep from the flock then separate and tend to it, just as Jesus was said to have caught up sinners from the throng to minister to them. Then it all went wrong quite quickly. It got a bit crazy as the less than pious Princes of the Church transformed the deliberately humble crook into a fashion accessory. The Crosier became the ultimate Holy bling.

The bishops and abbots of old were wealthy men, ostentatious men, far removed from the reality of the lives of most of their congregations, and they were big on visible wealth. The basic Shepherd's Crook style was known as a pedum but as time went by it was personalised and pimped-up with precious metals, ornate carvings and fat jewels. So in the 11th and 12th Centuries we see a phantasmagorical explosion of designs and expensive materials used on Crosiers. A far cry indeed from their Saviour's preaching and a world away from the trials and tribulations of their congregations especially those with illness or disability. In those times the Church didn't provide pews or any seating at all for worshippers and so those who relied on crutches for support were forced to 'go to the wall' to find a place to lean. That expression is still used today for companies that go bust. They go to the wall. It's fair to say that rarely happened to Bishops.

In time another form of Bishops' staff developed which saw the curved crook sacrificed to make way for a knob on top of the staff, surmounted by a crucifix. It was called a Ferula or Cambuta and again allowed for more artistic expression in the form of gold, silver and precious stones. These Ferula were much favoured by the Popes until the 13th Century when it's pretty clear the Papacy thought Ferula were no longer exclusive enough. There were just too many of them floating about Abbeys and Cathedrals and the medieval Popes no longer deigned to carry such a commonplace symbol; not that it made those symbols any less popular with the rest of the church hierarchy. Yet a third style was called a Crux Decussate, which often had two serpents battling on a top of a T-shaped staff. This was also known a Crocia and was popular in the Eastern tradition of the Orthodox Church. Originally made from cypress wood it soon began to appear in ivory, gold and silver as wealthy prelates sought to bedazzle their flocks.

All the while a bizarre etiquette was developing around the carriage and deportment of Crosiers because there's nothing those old Bishops liked more than a bit of posturing ritual. So, in the days when Ferula were still in favour the Popes would carry one that had three bars on its cross, one more than those on an Archbishop's. And a Bishops Crosier seemingly outgunned an Abbott's so if an Abbot found himself in the presence of a Crosier-toting bishop he was obliged to cover the crook on his own Crosier with a cloth. Unusually in such a male dominated world Abbesses were allowed to carry a Crosier too but only in the presence of their nuns.

Because of their love of precious metals, particularly silver, on the shaft of the Crosier there was also a fashion for cloths called sudariums (literally sweat cloths) to keep the Bishops' clammy palms from discolouring their shafts. And as the cult of the Crosier developed there was a strict code of when and where they could be used and even the way in which they could be properly carried. All this was codified in a book published in 1600 by Pope Clement VIII, called the Caeremoniale Episcoporum; the Ceremonials of Bishops. It instructs Bishops they should always carry the Crosier with the crook facing the congregation or the altar but never facing the bishop himself. There's actually quite a bit more Crosier etiquette but I think it's best if I spare you the mind-numbing details.

What particularly interests me about Crosiers are the powerful dragon or serpent motifs found on a great many of them. Some depict a cross piercing a serpent others the Archangel Michael or St. George smiting a dragon. Do we really accept that our forbears believed in dragons and giant serpents? I certainly don't but I believe these enigmatic decorations tell us an altogether different and far more sinister story. I believe they represent the triumph of Christianity over the last outposts of the Druid religion in post-Roman Europe and I don't think this was a religious coup achieved without bloodshed. I suspect it was a full on religious cleansing.

Let me tell you something about the Druids or at least what we know of them that is relevant to our Christian Crosiers. I've already touched on the Druid belief in metempsychosis, a sort of early take on Quantum Theory relying on the existence of multiple dimensions, but the Druids were also wrapped-up in the cult of snakes. They were Ophites like the Ancient Egyptians but the Druids never wrote down any of their religious knowledge or practices believing that would taint and dilute their ancient beliefs. Instead they learnt it all by rote, including their systems of geometry and astronomy, taking anything up to twenty years or more to become proficient. We know this from Roman sources, particularly Julius Caesar himself, and from the writings of the last of the Bards of Wales and Ireland who tried to pass on some of the Druid knowledge in coded poems before Christians swept it away with the power of their own written word held in the Bible.

One fact about the Druids is absolutely striking. The original Welsh language of the Iron Age is known as Brythonic Welsh and in this ancient language there is a word 'gnadr.' It means both serpent and Druid. In Brythonic Welsh they are one and the same because to those people Adder and Druid were synonymous. The implication is clear. Serpent cults were central to the Celtic forms of worship and to the ceremonies of their Druid priests who were said to carry staffs decorated with snake emblems.

Enter a teenager called Maewyn who was captured by pirates on the Welsh coast around 370AD and sold as a slave in Ireland where he worked as a shepherd boy before escaping and returning to mainland Britain. He was to return to Ireland transformed into a zealous Christian missionary who'd taken the name Patricius and used his knowledge of Ireland and its language to help in his mission. He was destined to become St. Patrick and a biography of his life written by a monk, says the Druid's had eerily foretold his coming in a prophetic rhyme, which referred to his Crosier and his religious fervour.

'Across the sea will come adze-head, crazed in the head,
His cloak with hole for the head, his stick bent in the head.'

Many miracles have been attributed to the Patron Saint of Ireland but perhaps the most famous relates to the day he drove all the snakes on the island of Ireland into the sea using his Crosier, his 'stick bent in the head' to banish them. The fact is there has never been any species of snake native to Ireland simply because the Ice Age and the Irish Sea, which formed when the ice sheet retreated, were natural barriers that prevented snakes ever colonising Ireland. Natural history experts at the National Museum of Ireland say there aren't even any snake fossils in the Irish geological record. Quite simply there have never been any snakes in Ireland that weren't in a zoo or a pet shop. But of course it's not reptiles the legend of St. Patrick refers too. It's those other 'snakes' he drove out of Ireland, those other adders, the 'gnadr,' when he killed off the local Druids. I suspect what happened was this. Once Patrick had converted enough of the local population to Christianity, no doubt a powerful king or two as well, then he would have turned them against the Druids who would have been dealt with brutally and terminally. In the same way the dragon slaying by St. George and the Archangel Michael were also metaphors for the slaying of those human serpents, the Druids, who were once present across much of Western Europe. They were finishing the work begun in Gaul and on Anglesey by the Romans.

I think this largely undocumented and violent religious purging, only ever referred to by the Church in metaphors, was probably more widespread across the British Isles than we'll ever know. I've no doubt the Christian missionaries who orchestrated it deliberately hid their deeds of genocide behind the metaphors of St. George and the Dragon or Patrick and the Snakes because they simply didn't want to acknowledge there'd ever been another belief system before them. They stamped out the Druids then tried to write them out of history. And if you look hard enough you'll find more evidence of this attack on the 'Old Religion' on the British mainland too. Tucked away in a stunning corner of the Wiltshire countryside is a massive Stone Circle that completely encompasses the medieval village of Avebury built in its confines. The Avebury Stone Circle is so huge and so significant it's listed as a World Heritage Site; a special place indeed. I know it well. I live a short drive away.

Just on the edge of the Circle itself you'll find the Avebury Parish Church of St. James, which was originally built by Saxons at the auspicious turning of the millennium in 1000AD. Inside the Church, under the bell tower, you'll find an ancient stone 'tub font' large enough to perform total immersion baptisms. It is carved, rather crudely, although the imagery is plain, and it's reckoned to date from the 11th Century but I wouldn't be surprised if it were a bit older. It's those carvings that tell a long forgotten story of Avebury as they depict a man with a cross on his chest, carrying a book that is surely the Bible in his left hand and wielding a Crosier in his right. He is stamping down on two large serpents at his feet; two more 'gnadr' being put to death.

Historians have dismissed out of hand legends linking Stone Circles like Avebury and Stonehenge to the Druids but the truth is we don't know how long the secret practice of Druidism lasted on the Islands of Britain. If you accept that the 'snakes' referred to in Patrick's story were Druids as I do then they were here at least until the 4th Century AD. And if the ancient beliefs were still being practiced on the mainland then surely a place like Avebury would have been natural focus for their worship.

Historians may say there's no evidence linking Druid worship to Stone Circles. I beg to differ but that's a subject for another book. In any event the Avebury font suggests something had indeed gone down. I can easily imagine Christian priests in the fifth and sixth centuries uncovering Druid worshippers clinging on to their old practices in a place like Avebury then stamping on them just as the carving on the font depicts.

And I believe the same thing happened in the strange case of Radnor Forest just inside the Welsh border near the town of Presteigne. Legend has it the last Dragon in Wales is confined in the forest and guess what, it's kept imprisoned there by five churches which surround the mountainous area and inscribe the shape of a pentangle on the landscape. Stephanie and I drove up there in the summer of 2018. It's a beautiful area, more moorland than wood, and the churches tucked in its folds are beautiful too.

No surprise, to us at any rate, that all five of those churches are named St. Michael or Llanfihangel in Welsh, after the serpent slaying Archangel. And neither will you be surprised to hear that my suspicion is the early Christians in Radnor Forest found a group of people still practicing the old Druid religion in the forest. They crushed them then reacted with a frenzy of church building, a chain of churches in fact, to manacle the dragon within. Stephanie and I wound or way to one of the St. Michaels of the Forest, Llanfihangel Discoed, which is built on an extraordinary site with a massive yew tree, reckoned to be five thousand years old, in its grounds together with a bubbling spring. The two vital elements of a Druid grove of course and I have no doubt the Old Religion was practiced there before Christ was born. Admirably these days the church building is used for community projects and art exhibitions, which help to keep its fabric maintained. Inside the church is one stunning, modern addition of a stained glass window at the western end, installed in 2017 in memory of a parishioner. It is a lyrical interpretation of the church in a winter landscape designed by an artist who strikingly portrays the phases of the moon, sequentially above the church. Wonderful. I have no idea what inspired the artist to this design but I can't help wondering whether the spirits of the ancient grove, where moon worshipping rites once took place, have caste their spell and whispered in the artist's ear from down the ages. Poignantly there was a rather fine hazel stick leaning against the wall in the porch of the church probably left there by a forgetful walker and we left it standing timeless in that place.

You may have gathered I see the ornate stick that is the Bishops' Crosier as symbolizing the worst excesses of the Church and the antithesis of sanctity. Inquisitions, burnings at the stake and burdensome abbey taxes levied on poor farmers were all carried out behind the authority of the Crosier. But I don't let that intense dislike cloud my vision and I'm not about to let the Druids off the hook either. Instead I'll turn to the sticks that were woven into the hideous Wicker Man; a legendary Celtic engine of human sacrifice.

There are a few historical references to human sacrifice by the Druids but only two references to the Wicker Man; one by Julius Caesar, the other by the early geographer Strabo. Caesar introduced us to the Wicker Man in his book on the Gallic Wars:

> *"They (the Celts) believe, in effect, that, unless for a man's life a man's life be paid, the majesty of the immortal gods may not be appeased; and in public, as in private life they observe an ordinance of sacrifices of the same kind. Others use figures of immense size whose limbs, woven out of twigs, they fill with living men and set on fire, and the men perish in a sheet of flame. They believe that the execution of those who have been caught in the act of theft or robbery or some crime is more pleasing to the immortal gods; but when the supply of such fails they resort to the execution even of the innocent."*

In his Geographia Strabo talks about the Druids and human sacrifice and he mentions the giant figure of a 'straw and wood' man too:

> *"The Romans put a stop to customs connected with sacrifice and divination as they were in conflict with our own ways; for example they would strike a man who had been consecrated for sacrifice in the back with a sword, and make prophecies based on his death spasms and they would not sacrifice without the presence of the Druids. Other kinds of human sacrifice have been reported as well: some men they would shoot dead with arrows and impale in the temples: or they would construct a huge figure of straw and wood, and having thrown cattle and all manner of wild animals and humans into it, they would make a burnt offering of the whole thing."*

Sticks to make the Wicker Man and sticks to light it. What a terrifying way to go to your death although quite a few historians dismiss this as Roman propaganda against the Celts they so loathed. The victors get to tell history their way these experts argue. I don't agree. There is direct archaeological evidence of human sacrifice by Druidic peoples, not least the 'bog bodies' found in Ireland and the famous Lindow Man from Cheshire. These 'sacrifices' were men of apparently high status who were struck on the head before their throats were cut and their bodies thrown into the mire. Consigning a man to the bog would have great significance to those Iron Age Celts who believed in the liminal space between earthly life and the world of the Gods. Hence they made offerings of prized weapons and ornate jewellery thrown into streams and rivers; water being a liminal dimension. A bog might be liminal in their minds too but not the sparkling dimension of a stream, rather a muddy, sullied and terrifying one suitable to accept a sacrifice.

There are also numerous examples of human sacrifices made to bless a new Celtic home then buried in the footings of the house. These 'foundation sacrifices' are certainly not something the average council Building Inspector would countenance these days. So the Celts, who were enthusiastic head-hunters in battle by the way, definitely practiced human sacrifice and I can't think that Caesar's imagination was so vivid as to come up with the of the concept of the Wicker Man on its own; not unless he'd had a very bad nightmare. And to add considerable weight to the Roman contention of the Wicker Man there are some allusions to death by fire in the Irish and Welsh legends, especially the Mabinogion, where men are tricked into a specially constructed house, which is then set alight. Not so fundamentally different to the idea of the Wicker man is it? Anyway something deep within my Celtic soul shudders and my blood runs cold when I think about the aspect of a fiery giant consuming humans in his own flames.

Once again in fairness to the Romans those Iron Age Celts also employed impalement as a punishment. We know Boudicca certainly did and in Bavarian Germany at Holzhausen a deeply disturbing Iron Age shaft was found with a sharpened pole at the bottom, which carried traces of human flesh and blood. There's another Celtic impaling pit at Garton Slack in Yorkshire, wide at the top but narrowing to a wooden stake at the bottom. A young man and a woman, both aged around thirty, were found huddled around the stake. Presumably they'd both been thrown down but one had missed the impaling post only to die in misery at the bottom of the shaft. The poor woman cast into that hellhole had been pregnant at the time and a tiny fetal skeleton was discovered near her pelvis. What their crime had been the Gods only know.

Which brings us anything but neatly to the nastiest exponent of the sharpened stick of them all, a Transylvanian Count known as Vlad the Impaler, a man credited with running out of stakes because he'd impaled so many victims. Most of them were Muslims from the Ottoman Empire, which ran up against Vlad's territories in modern day Romania. Vlad, who was a member of the Dracula family, had a chequered career, which included a spell in a dungeon during which time it's said he caught rats and impaled them on sticks just to keep his hand in. Without going into all the gruesome details suffice it to say Vlad enjoyed his calling and is even credited with eating his supper on a table set amongst a forest of freshly adorned stakes.

Strange to say his appalling form of execution caught on with Vlad's own enemies. In time the Ottoman Empire took on impalement as their chosen punishment for any treasonable activities. Some poor souls took up to eight days to die in this way and if that isn't a deterrent then I don't know what is. There are other Sinister Sticks but the exposition of all this immolation and impaling is weary work and I feel like hurrying on to brighter, less blood soaked pastures.

Chapter 5
SPORTY STICKS

How would sport be without sticks I wonder? Very different that's for sure. There'd be no racehorses 'jumping over the sticks' at the Grand National, no footballs fired 'between the sticks' by goal scoring heroes during the World Cup. The fact of the matter is that sticks are everywhere in sport ranging from those used in Stick and Ball games to the humble yet vital sticks that hold up the flags marking the corners of a pitch. This is quite apart from the sports that are directly inspired by sticks like the javelin, which channels ancient prowess with a spear or the pole vault, simulating the skills needed to leap over a defensive ditch, a fortress wall or to cross a stream. And what could be more thrilling than a four by four hundred relay race in athletics events when the baton is passed from one team member to another? We all hold our breath when our teams are at the changeovers and pray the baton won't be dropped in a race that harks back to ancient messengers relaying urgent missives held on a Cleft Stick.

Equestrian sports are stick rich with show jumping requiring fences constructed from poles and cross-country eventing needs a lot of birch sticks in bundles too. Before horses are allowed to race on a course in the UK the Stewards of the course must assess the 'going,' which is an estimate of how soft or hard the ground is on the day of a race. Traditionally they would poke the turf with a walking stick to see how deep it would penetrate the ground beneath then make a judgement. The 'going' is important as some horses are physically better suited to 'heavy going' when hooves sink deeper and others prefer firm ground and so on. These days a high-tech electronic 'going stick' does the job introducing a degree of scientific rigour to a process, which after all has a lot of money riding on it.

Sticks then are an integral part of the horsey scene to an extent that took me completely aback while researching this book. Picture for a moment a sports hall with jumps, perhaps I should call them hurdles, laid out in a complex pattern. There's a holding ring where the contestants, almost exclusively teenage girls, pace around warming up their mounts. It's at this point it all gets a bit whacky as these young equestrians are dressed in running gear and their mounts are hobbyhorses. Yes, that's right they're riding the traditional children's toys that feature a padded model of a horse's head on a stick. The idea is to compete with pretend horses as if they are at an event with real horses so the youngsters race over the jumps incurring penalty points for knocking down fences as they complete their round. A clear round on their hobbyhorse is what they're after. They even compete at dressage holding their 'horses' proud as they imitate the stylised, high stepping movements of a fully trained dressage horse.

I know that senior event riders, who obviously compete on real horses, have taken hobbyhorses into the ring to entertain spectators during a break in competition. And it's become a bit of a thing to do for fun on the US rodeo riding circuit too. Whether the 'real' riders got the idea from the Scandinavian girls or the other way round I have no idea. But one thing's for certain, the romance of the hobbyhorse has a powerful effect on the teenage girls of Scandinavia especially in Finland where they've taken it to the next level.

It's become a major sport with ten thousand participants and an annual national championship featuring a couple of hundred of the best riders. I confess I've only seen videos of 'stick riding' as it's often called and to be fair it looks like an athletic sport requiring a high degree of fitness. However there is a culture within the sport that I can only describe as anti-anthropomorphism with girls pretending their hobbyhorses are real, tacking them up before a ride, assigning them bloodlines and even 'rugging' them before they sleep. Bella Swan from Twilight going National Velvet is the only analogy that comes readily to mind.

I started with the assumption that Scandinavian girls took to the world of the hobbyhorse because of a shortage of real ponies to ride in the Land of the Midnight Sun. However Scandinavian friends assure me there's definitely no shortage of horses and ponies because of the icy winters. Indeed hobbyhorses have always been a really popular toy and have probably endured better down the years in Scandinavia than in the UK. I've decided I won't be rushing to add a visit to the Finnish Hobbyhorse championship to my bucket list but the teens of Turku have wakened memories of a Saturday ritual when my daughter Alice was in her teens. She was pony mad at the time and loved to go to a local riding school where she would show jump in an indoor school. That's all she wanted to do. She didn't want to go out on hacks across the countryside; all she wanted was the challenge of those horizontal sticks. Alice would fall off and just get back on the horse again showing signs of the steely determination she can display, sometimes to my terror if we clash over politics. It seemed natural to ask Alice, a thoroughly modern young woman who is deputy editor of an online video gaming magazine, what she thought of the hobbyhorse craze. "Hmmm, let me think about it and I'll get back to you."

A couple of days later she called, "I don't think it's that weird. I mean maybe the form is, but the impulse is pretty universal. It's just playing. And teens and adults like doing that too, it's just seen as less acceptable the older you get. So if there's an outlet for it that's sort of allowed, I get that people would really be into it like the people who play Quidditch, the sport from Harry Potter played on broomsticks, in real life."

"Oh, I didn't know that," said I. But sure enough there is a band of hardy wizard types who race about with customized broomsticks between their legs whacking a ball and Alice is right, it's not so different from those Scandinavian hobbyhorse riders. There are about twenty thousand Quidditch players in twenty-five countries and a clearly defined book of rules filled with Potteresque terminology to regulate a fairly roughhouse sport with mixed gender teams.

After considering these quite eccentric Stick Sports I'm coming to the belief that flights of sporting imagination, including video gaming, sprang up among a population of young people who crave some magic in their lives. We live in an age where science and technology make the spellbinding seem prosaic so little wonder young people seek out their own enchantments and if they can't find it they invent it for themselves. And why not?

Of course more mainstream sports produce their own magic too conjured up by the almost supernatural skills of the best players; men and women who harness time and space and do with it what they will. Without doubt there's also something of the warlike in the competitive element of sport especially at an international level; war and magic are an ageless combination. The fans of particular clubs, be it football, hurling, baseball or countless other sports, happily take on a tribal identity in their support that seems to satisfy a deep-seated need for community.

I'm a Welsh rugby fan and I keenly feel the residue of past battles and ancient enmities when my national team plays England during the Six Nations tournament. These occasions generate great fervour but happily, in the case of rugby at least, conflict among rival spectators is so rare as to be inconsequential. However I remember another sporting occasion when there wasn't even a sniff of good will in the air as I covered one of my most surreal assignments as a correspondent. It was back in 1982 and my news editor at the Daily Express told me, "Al, you're booked on a flight to Lisbon."

"Okay boss, what's happening out there?"

"It's the World Roller Hockey Championships."

"Never heard of roller hockey boss and anyway I'm not a sports writer."

"It's hockey played on roller skates, pretty obvious I thought," he sniffed, "And we need a news man out there because England are playing the Argentine this week."

My news editor didn't have to say any more. As I say it was 1982 and a time when the UK and the Argentine were at war over the occupation of the Falkland Islands. Those world championships had long been scheduled and to say passions were running high is a bit of an understatement. Frankly I was surprised the fixture went ahead at all but if it hadn't then the whole championship would have been abandoned. So, after some torrid negotiations, both sides agreed to play on but there'd be no shaking of hands or exchanging of national pennants. Ten men flying around a hockey rink wielding sticks while their nations were at war; what could possibly go wrong? Fellow Welshman, good friend and Daily Mail rival John Edwards, was on the same flight and, if memory serves, the match took place a day after a British submarine sank the Argentine battleship Belgrano with the loss of three hundred and twenty three of her crew.

The fixture was played in a large sports hall and I remember the English chaps cruising around waiting for the Argentine team to come out. Oh dear, when they did I swear steam was coming out of their Latin American ears and their roller blades were crackling and sparking with static. In my subsequent piece I remember writing the Argentines were so pumped up they were 'flexing the muscles in their eyelids.' There's no doubt they were a different class to the English team and went on to demolish them eight goals to nil as Argentine sticks flashed through the air hitting lumps out of the Brits. Afterwards the Argentine Ambassador told his team, "Today you have won a war!"

He wasn't wrong and as we walked away from the stadium the usually garrulous John Edwards was uncharacteristically thoughtful. "What's up John?" I asked.

"Nothing really Al, I was just thinking it's a bloody good job the only sticks we have in rugby are the posts." He wasn't wrong either. When I told Stephanie this story I learnt something new about my partner; a woman of many surprises. She was completely unfazed as she'd often played roller hockey for fun with friends in San Francisco and told me, "I've still got my stick somewhere."

That game of roller hockey between two nations at war had been a battle of sorts though in the circumstances it had been quite restrained to the extent that none of the players had been hospitalised. But there's another stick game that was once played out with the ferocity of a real battle. These days it's particularly popular in expensive private schools where it's thought to be 'character building.' We call it Lacrosse but the fiercely proud Native tribes of North America, whose game it was originally, have their own name for it, which translates as 'Little Brother of War.' And according to accounts from the first settlers in the forest draped mountains and valleys of Canada and New England that name perfectly sums it up.

These days the formalised, rule-encompassed game of Lacrosse, played by ten men or women on each side, bears no resemblance at all to the magnificent spectacle that once unfolded in the pristine valleys of North America. In those days it was played with a heavy stick and basket of hickory and rawhide that modern players with their super light carbon fibre jobs would find well nigh impossible to wield. Algonquin, Huron, the Five Nations of the Iroquois -Mohawk, Onondaga, Oneida, Cayuga and Seneca – the Mohicans, Choctaws, Micmacs and countless other tribal groups would gather for games sometimes lasting a week or more. And these weren't just games in the recreational sense because those Original People played as an offering to the Creator who had given them the game as a gift. In return to play well, to make poetry with stick and ball, was their greatest gift to the gods.

What a perfect symmetry of belief and they did it in great style! There are reports of gatherings of one hundred thousand people turning out to watch and play in games that meandered over the landscape in a seemingly violent chaos; unless of course you were a player. One hundred thousand tribal people, think of it. And when you do think too of this, at present there are only one hundred thousand people of the Five Nations of the Iroquois still surviving; from glorious game to genocide. I can't begin to imagine the shame of it. It's wonderful then that a strong spark survives. Although we Europeans all but wiped out the tribes, young Iroquois men still play the game in heart-lifting places like Onondaga Community College in Upper New York State. On the Onondaga team website I found videos of some of those inspirational young men using words like 'sacred' and 'healing' when they talk of a contest that they believe cleanses their spirits.

In any event games involving ten thousand men, proud and painted, with their attendant feasts and ceremonies, were said to still be common when Europeans first arrived in America. They hooked and hurled the ball with whoops and shrieks. Can you imagine the scene? It must have been fantastic and I'd like to think their ghosts are still whooping on the playing fields along the banks of the mighty Hudson and Connecticut, the St. Lawrence and the fair Housatonic where the Mohicans lived.

Another inspiring story of a stick sport held sacred by the native people, this time a little closer to home, is in Ireland where the game of hurling was once played to celebrate the Gods at the sacred sites of the Celtic tribes. I've watched a game or rather winced at a game, as hurling is played with an intensity I think could fairly be described as The Little Brother of War too. Like its Native American counterpart the game of hurling is fast, furious and dangerous with sticks flashing, crashing and slapping on flesh. I've watched local hurling games in Ireland and wondered how anyone walked away in one piece.

Hurling has its roots deep in the mists of Irish pre-history. There's evidence that a game similar in description was played at the sites of great Irish cultural centres like the Ancient Hill of the Kings at Tara. There are descriptions of it in the enigmatic Bardic epic of the Tain Bo Cuailigne, The Cattle Raid of Culee, and another Bardic tome called the Book of the Dun Cow. It lifts my spirit to think those ancient Irish warriors would have felt quite at home among the tribes of the Great Lakes and Rivers. Somehow I can see them on the day of a game, painted blue with woad, holding feasts and sacrifices and calling for a cleansing from their deities just like the Five Nations of the Iroquois.

Some years before that roller hockey debacle in Lisbon I was assigned to cover a hostage taking for my newspaper (I was a reporter with the Daily Mail at the time) just outside the town of Kildare in the Irish Republic. Two rogue IRA members had kidnapped a rather charming Dutch guy called Tiede Herrema who was running a manufacturing company in the area. The IRA couple, Eddie Gallagher and Marian Coyle, were discovered holding their captive in a house on the edge of a hurling pitch in a little place called Monastarevin and the Irish authorities laid siege to the place for eighteen days. In total Dr Herrema was held hostage for thirty-six days. It has to be recorded that I was working with the same John Edwards at the time although he was a lot senior to me and got a free pass from the editor to leave the siege and fly to Cardiff where he watched the Wales v England rugby international. All right for some.

Anyway us media types had set up base in an encampment of hired caravans on one side of the pitch, the siege house was on the other and the Irish Army cordon lay between the two. Pretty quickly I discovered the locals were furious with Eddie and Marian for two very good reasons. First, Dr Herrema was providing a lot of people with jobs in his factory and they thought a Dutchman was definitely a neutral in the ages old conflict between the Irish and the English. Second, the army's activities were cutting their hurling field to ribbons and they blamed the rogue IRA duo's actions for the poor condition of their pitch. They didn't like that at all.

Thankfully it all ended without anyone coming to any harm and I can remember watching Eddie and Marian exhausted and in shreds when they were led away by the police. Dr Herrema, not so much. In fact he was quite good humoured and relaxed when he gave a press conference the following day and declared it had been a bit of a picnic compared to when he'd been a Dutch Resistance fighter and the Gestapo had arrested him, brutally interrogated him and sent him to a concentration camp in Poland. It was deeply ironic then that Eddie and Marian had done so little research into their kidnapping project they believed Dr Herrema was in fact a German. So it was that my first experience of a hurling field saw me introduced to a hero and two clowns. Later when I watched a game of hurling I thought the players were hard, brave sporting heroes, if a little foolish to be messing with those sticks. It was also evident to me that quite a few of them looked as though they'd have been just as happy taking on the opposition with their traditional club, the shillelagh, in their hands.

Tough sports indeed but then there's the Donga, which takes sporting sticks to another uncompromising level. I've only ever seen films of this sport cum right of passage but even viewed on screen it's a wincing, painful watch as young Suri warriors of the Ethiopian highlands whack and crack each other without mercy. It's a sort of inter-village competition as young men set out to prove they are brave and skilled enough to run their own cattle herd in the dangerous, lion infested bush.

It's also a flirt-fest with the most beautiful young women in the area vying to attract the attention of the fighters and, of course, vice versa. However the fight itself is a crazy confusion of totally naked and seemingly fearless young men trying to hit each other senseless with ten-foot long sticks. I say totally naked but they are allowed some negligible head protection and laughably small knuckle protectors made of basketry. More important is what they don't have and that's a box to protect their genitalia which are frequently injured much too the dismay of the beauties on the sideline one imagines. There is a real danger of death in the Donga so don't try it at home.

Interestingly this 'sport' seems to go with the cattle herding culture so there are variations on stick fighting right across Southern Africa encompassing the Masai and Zulu tribes too. In South Africa it's called Nguni and as a young boy tending the family herd Nelson Mandela was an exponent of stick fighting. It goes some way to explaining the courage and fortitude of the great man who spent twenty-seven years in prison only to show those who imprisoned him such magnanimity when he was released.

Perhaps the most arcane, almost mystical aspect of stick games is the actual sourcing of the sticks. To me it's inconceivable that the act of making a lacrosse racket or a hurling stick in the days of the tribes would not have been a sacred undertaking. After all they were destined to play games dedicated to the gods. And though times change the making of bats and sticks still carries a spiritual reverence connected to the secrets of the craft. It starts with the sourcing of the best trees for the wood that's needed. Most bats and sticks are made from trees that have been coppiced or encouraged to grow in a particular way. If they are not carefully tended they will grow side shoots that will cause knots in the wood and so they're literally not top notch, an expression that originally comes from the forests of New England and Appalachia where the stocks that are used to make baseball bats are grown. Traditionally they were made from ash trees but in the 1990's a new trend for making bats from maple wood began. Just as well really because two years into the new millennium scientists discovered an Asian beetle boring its way into American ash trees. By 2016 the voracious Emerald Ash Borer had munched its way through an estimated fifty million ash trees in the United States making maple the sensible choice for baseball bats.

A hurley is the name given to the stick used to play the game of hurling and recently, whilst writing this book, I was told a tale of secret visits to the glades of an English forest by Irish craftsmen looking for top grade ash stocks to make hurleys. The forest lies near my home but I promised not to name its location. You see the native Irish Ash is so scarce the Irish are forced to make forays into English woods in a quest for the best stocks for their sticks. A friend, who must also remain nameless, told me that a particular stand of ash trees in this forest is quite brutally coppiced almost to the ground to create strong, straight growths with bulbous connections to the trunk just below the surface. It takes at least fifteen years to grow a set of stocks around a particular bole and then he told me, "Every few years an Irishman arrives, pays top money, then takes a chainsaw to the base of one of the coppiced trees. He ruins a couple of chains doing it because he's cutting beneath the soil but he doesn't mind as he's getting the best quality ash for his hurling sticks."

Long may it last because the native English Ash, like its American cousin, is also under threat from a different invasive species, a fungus called Hymenoscyphus fraxineus commonly known as Ash Dieback. It arrived in the UK around 2012 and is killing a lot of trees. Fortunately ash trees are prolific multipliers, to the point where my farmer friend John Kerr calls them 'the weed tree', and because of this resistant strains have already been identified. I hope so. I rather like the symmetry of an Irish Hurley craftsman making a pilgrimage to an English forest to keep an ancient Celtic game alive.

There's another sport where the sticks they use are held in great veneration. It's also the sport that has the more participants than any other. It's called Fishing or Angling. In the UK alone over five million people actually take part in this recreational pastime quite apart from those who fish for a living. A lot more people watch football or rugby but nowhere near as many actually play those games. The term Angling comes from the Old German word for fishing hook 'angg' and long before it became a recreation it was a vital source of sustenance. Fish were netted, stabbed with spears or caught with hooks made of bones or crafted seas shells. Examples of hooks nearly twenty three thousand years old have been found in a cave on the Japanese island of Okinawa. But this is the Book of Sticks not the Book of Hooks and it's the delivery system we are interested in.

Originally baited hooks were simply thrown on a line into a stream and hauled back in if a fish took the bait and got hooked. Then someone had the idea of attaching the hook and line to a stick to get the all-important bait further out over the water to lure the fish onto the hook. Then somewhere along the line someone who definitely wasn't a peasant decided luring a fish with an artificial fly on a hook was a relaxing pastime. Most authorities believe fly-fishing was born sometime around the 14th or 15th Century and was definitely the preserve of nobles only. I'm not so sure about that time frame as the legend of the Fisher King, the last Keeper of the Holy Grail, is a lot older and has him wounded in the groin and spending his time fishing on the lake near his castle while he waited for a cure. At any rate it seems to have continued as a 'nobility only' sport until the English Civil War ended and Izaak Walton wrote his celebrated description of fly-fishing, The Compleat Angler. This made little difference to the demographic enjoying the sport except that its preserve was extended to include 'gentlemen' as well as the aristocracy. It was only in the middle of the 20th Century when working men had some leisure time did the sport of fishing explode. Not fly fishing for trout and salmon it has to be said, which was still cornered by rich folk, but coarse fishing for carp, tench, bream and pike instead. That attracted millions of weekend anglers and still does. For those who practice it the best quality fly-fishing rods are still made from those expensive sticks called split cane. It's also true that fly fishermen, and increasingly women, use staffs to keep their balance when they wade into the rush of the river, a wading stick, and a heavy, weighted stick called a priest to deliver the last rites to any fish they catch.

These days synthetic materials like metal alloys and carbon fibre rule the banks of fishing lakes and rivers but when I was a youngster back home in Wales we would use another stick, knocked into the river bank, to hold a baited hook on a 'nightline' left overnight to be hauled in next day hopefully with a fish on the end. I'm told this is poaching but I was too young to understand that back in the day; at least that's my story and I'm sticking to it. As I've mentioned I live on the banks of an English river these days and watch the fishermen casting their flies onto the gin clear waters of the chalk stream with a patience that is lost on me. Still they enjoy themselves and I know they love their rods and value them beyond their monetary worth, which is considerable.

My riverbank home is some thirty miles away from the town of Andover where there's a wonderful tourist attraction that doubles as a conservation haven for threatened species of raptors in particular vultures so close to total extinction they are on the Red List. It's called the Hawk Conservancy and I first took my eldest son Harry there when he was about five. He loved it and, after studying at Oxford, working as a publisher and finally landing at the National Theatre, he still does. Harry unashamedly declares he will never grow out of his love for a day at the Hawk Conservancy and is a big fan of Ashley Smith who ran the place for years but has since retired to the Highlands of Scotland. Harry loved Ashley's informed and funny commentaries to the absolutely stunning flying displays they put on most days of the year. In fact Harry loves the place to the point where he recently called me to say my birthday present would be arriving by e-mail.

"It's a sort of selfish present," he said.

"What do you mean? What is it?" I asked.

"A thirty quid voucher for the Hawk Conservancy," said Harry, "And obviously I'll be one of the people redeeming it."

He didn't need to say any more as I love the place too and what better present for a father than to revisit a place of long-standing, fond memories with his son. Harry couldn't make it until quite recently when we used my voucher to have a rain sodden but lovely fix for his addiction. However, a month or two after receiving my present I took Stephanie for her first visit and as I'd predicted she was absolutely blown away by the displays and the sheer love shown for the birds in their care. One of the tableaus portrayed the medieval sport of falconry. I'd seen it before but what a delight when my favourite set of sporting sticks was described by one of the Conservancy's presenters. It's called a Cadge.

In common English slang you can 'cadge' a lift off someone, or cadge the price of a pint. It's come to mean to 'scrounge or beg' but the root of that phrase lies with the rectangular wooden frame, originally a set of poles lashed together, that a falconer's servant would use to carry the birds around the hunting ground. The 'cadger' as he was called would step into the centre of the frame as it lay on the ground then lift it by two leather straps onto his shoulders.

On this frame the cadger would set out his Peregrines to perch until such time as the nobleman who'd retained him needed the birds to hunt. What a wonderful set of sticks is the cadge, a mobile eyrie for the most noble of the scything raptors. And there the falcon waits; fierce eyes covered by a calming hood, until the leather jesses anchoring it to the firmament are slipped. Then the prince of the skies, flight feathers stiff, can soar, stoop, exhilarate; no need to cadge a lift.

Chapter 6
POOH STICKS

We all know the story don't we. It begins when Winnie the Pooh is walking through the Hundred Acre Wood holding a fir cone in his paw as he tries to compose a poem about it but try as he might he can't find a rhyme. Then as he comes to a bridge over the stream the little bear trips and the cone falls and lands with a splash in the river.

'Bother,' says Pooh as he looks for another fir cone but changes his mind and decides to lie down and watch the river flow by. And that's when he sees his fir cone emerge from under the bridge and float away. It was a light bulb moment for Pooh! He'd dropped it on one side of the bridge but it had come out on the other. Will it work again he wonders and so he drops another cone into the water on the upstream side of the bridge and sure enough it floats out on the downstream side. Curiosity drives Pooh to try dropping two cones into the river at the same time and one emerges first but he can't tell which so he tries again with two fir cones of different sizes. As he'd suspected the bigger one was the first to emerge and he played the fir cone game all afternoon making thirty-six correct guesses and getting it wrong twenty eight times. There's another seminal moment when Pooh realises that he can play with sticks of the same size to tell them apart and as he rightly observes it's easier to say Pooh Sticks than Poohfircones and it goes like this:

> Narrator: Now one day, Pooh and Piglet, Rabbit and Roo were all playing Pooh sticks together.

> Pooh: But why do we call it Pooh sticks? I thought I started with fir cones.

> Narrator: You did, Pooh, but sticks are easier to mark. [Pooh thinks to himself, then smiles]

> Pooh: Oh, yes, now I remember.

So A. A. Milne's charming evocation of the world of the One Hundred Acre woods, which has enthralled generations of children, gave birth to a whimsical, serendipitous pastime, the game of Poohsticks. All you need is flowing water, a bridge, some sticks, some friends, maybe mum and dad too, to while away the hours. It is the perfect game for little children and although they may move on to skipping stones and other less quaint pastimes they'll surely never grow out of Poohsticks.

Inevitably someone came up with the idea of a Poohsticks competition and for the past thirty-five years the World

Poohsticks Championships have been held at Whitney in Oxfordshire. There are individual and team categories and in 2018 a bloke from Oxford was crowned individual champion with a chap who'd come all the way from Washington USA as runner up. I'm not sure I wholeheartedly approve of competitive Poohsticks preferring a more lyrical approach to the pastime, which after all is hardly a skill-based sport. However the Whitney event is for charity and I'm sure Pooh and the gang wouldn't begrudge those good causes; not even for a pot of honey.

There is, however, a more contentious issue arising from the Oxfordshire location of the World Championships. They claim to the 'the home of Poohsticks' but hold on, there's a place that has a knock-out claim to that prestigious title and it's the Ashdown Forest in East Sussex. It's here that A. A. Milne set his adventure and placed the characters of Christopher Robin, based on his young son, the eponymous Christopher Robin, together with Pooh, Piglet and Eeyore. The Milne family lived at Cotchford Farm on the edge of a section of the forest called the Five Hundred Acre Wood and the author would often take his Christopher Robin walking there. The artist who sketched the famous illustrations for the books, E. H. Shepard, drew on the same forest for his inspiration and when Christopher Robin was asked about it as an adult he settled the matter, "Pooh's Forest and Ashdown Forest are identical."

Ashdown Forest has become a place of Pooh Pilgrimage and those who find their way to the village of Hartfield in East Sussex will soon find themselves in the locations made famous in the books; The Enchanted Place, Heffalump Trap, Eeyore's Sad and Gloomy Place and of course Pooh Bridge where our game was invented. If you go there remember to collect your sticks in the woods before you reach the bridge. Over the years thousands of Pooh Pilgrims used-up all the available sticks that lay nearby.

Time to take a deep breath and you'll need it as there are other, very different Pooh Sticks I want to tell you about and they are a world away from the timeless charm of Winnie the Pooh and the Hundred Acre Wood. Indeed they are entirely lavatory-centric to coin a phrase. You see the ancients of Classical Greece and Rome had some strange toilet habits; strange to us at least. Their lavatories were anything but privies as they did their business in communal toilets with seats, often made of stone, lined above running water. Toilet paper was not even on the radar back in those times so instead they chose to use a sea sponge on the end of a stick to wipe their bottoms clean. The Greeks called them xylospongium while the Romans called them tersorium. The tersorium was an intimate implement that was actually shared between users in the Roman public latrines. The drill was this. You'd do your business then use the sponge on a stick to wipe your bottom before rinsing it off in the running water of the loo. The tersorium was then placed in a jar containing salt water or vinegar as a rudimentary disinfectant to await the next user.

You might imagine the Emperor and the patrician classes had their own tersorium if indeed they didn't have a slave to wipe their bums for them. However the proletariat of ancient Rome might well have been less fastidious in their toilet habits and historians reckon their lavatories were breeding grounds for disease and infection. Who, for instance would want to follow a chap with an STI who'd just used the tersorium before you? That indeed would be the 'shitty end of the stick' as the saying goes, its origins in the Roman lavatory as is the root of the closely related saying, 'You've got the wrong end of the stick.'

The use of 'sponges on sticks' was illustrated on a wall mural in the Roman port of Ostia and it gets a mention here and there in classical writings too. But perhaps the most disturbing and moving story is the account written in the First Century by the historian Seneca about the particularly macabre death of an enslaved man.

> *"For example there was lately in a training school for wild-beast gladiators a German who was making himself ready for the morning exhibition; he withdrew in order to relieve himself – the only thing he was allowed to do without the presence of a guard.*
>
> *While so engaged he seized the stick of wood, tipped with a sponge, which was devoted to the vilest of uses and stuffed it, just as it was, down his throat. Thus he blocked up his windpipe and choked the breath from his body. That was truly an insult to death!"*

You can only try to imagine the hopelessness and futility of that poor man's life yet Seneca admired the manner of his death, and the release and ultimate freedom it gave the poor German gladiator, continuing:

> *"Yes indeed, it was not a very elegant or becoming way to die but what is more foolish than to be over-nice about dying? What a brave fellow! He surely deserved to be allowed to choose his fate. How bravely he would have wielded a sword (to end his life) With what courage he would have hurled himself into the depths of the sea or down a precipice.*
>
> *Cut off from resources on every hand, he yet found a way to furnish himself with death and with a weapon for death. Let each man judge the deed of this most zealous fellow as he likes, provided we agree on this point, that the foulest death is preferable to the fairest slavery."*

What a dreadful way to die. That story casts a shadow and makes me contemplate just how much torment and cruelty the human spirit can bear before it can take no more. Seneca does indeed prompt us into thinking about the nature and price of freedom and the horrors of slavery.

At this point I'll let my mind wander again to the endless plains and deserts of Central Asia where, for fifteen hundred years, the Silk Road carried trade to and from China and the West. This legendary caravan route conjures up names like those of Marco Polo the Italian explorer or the fabulous trading city of Samarkhand. The Silk Road was actually a network of routes across the Gobi Desert and the never-ending grasslands of Bactria through modern Iraq and Iran and then to Turkey on the borders of Europe. As its name suggests the most sought after commodity that travelled the Road was silk. The trade in silk actually began long before Marco Polo passed through the Great Wall of China in the 14th Century with its heyday in Roman times. The Romans loved silk clothing and a great deal of silk was taken to the Greek island of Kos where skilled women tailors transformed them into luxurious and quite often 'licentious' clothing in the eyes of more traditional Romans. With silk generating the trade a whole range of goods were carried both ways. Everything from hunting dogs to slaves, from glassware to Chinese ceramics was carried along the Silk Road.

Eventually in the middle of the 15th Century the rulers of the Ottoman Empire decided to close the route down as they were in conflict with Christian Europe. They couldn't have anticipated the result of that decision as, robbed of their landward trading route, the European powers took to the seas instead. So began the Age of Discovery as Westerners sailed across the oceans to find what they could no longer obtain along the Silk Road. Even so the Silk Road left posterity with a great legacy of cultural as well as commercial exchange.

Peoples from very different worlds were able to see and experience art, philosophy as well as different languages and architectures because of that tenuous thread of a road linking peoples across the continents. But the Silk Road bequeathed other more dreadful legacies not least of which was the arrival of gunpowder in Europe from China and we all know the explosion of death that caused in the wider world.

Then there were the epidemics. You see the traders of the Silk Road had more in common with the Romans than their love of the wonderful produce of the silkworm. They too enjoyed, if that's the word, a stick culture on the toilet. However their sticks did not include a sponge, which at least had the benefit of some form of disinfection however rudimentary. No, the caravan traders wound bits of cloth around the 'wrong end' of their stick and they too shared their bottom cleansing implements one with another.

Scientists have little doubt that bubonic plague left its home in the Far East and leapfrogged from bum to bum along the Silk Road to ravish the populations of Medieval Europe. The equally awful epidemics of anthrax and leprosy are thought to have bummed a lift along the Silk Road too. Then in 2018 two brilliant Cambridge researchers, Hui-Yuan Yeh and Piers Mitchell, found some empirical evidence of disease-transfer along the Silk Road from an archaeological dig that took place at a trading way station called Xuanquanzhi, in the desert of the Tamarin Basin, which is essentially a thousand mile from anywhere.

The actual dig took place twenty years ago and revealed some headline grabbing documents written on silk. But when anthropologist Hui-Yuan Yeh heard the latrines at Xuanquanzhi had also been excavated and a cluster of bamboo 'hygiene sticks' found she had a hunch they'd be at least as exciting as the silk manuscripts. Sure enough she and Piers

Mitchell found all sorts of parasitic eggs on the sticks but one in particular, Chinese liver fluke, only thrives in marshy areas. That meant it had to have come from China and if a parasite can travel the Silk Road so can a pathogen. The Cambridge duo had their breakthrough.

There's another Poo Stick and I only mention it because every man of a certain age should meet the wooden sticks that comes with a hospital bowel cancer testing kit. This is there to help you prepare your faeces for a screening test and everyone contacted about this programme should do themselves a favour and check. You know it makes sense.

I've nearly finished with Pooh Sticks and let's be fair, far better to dwell on A. A. Milne's charming story of the Hundred Acre Wood than splutter and urge over Seneca's story of the death of a gladiator. But there's just one more I'd like to mention. Remember the Aztecs' fondness for a bit of blowgun hunting in the forests of Central America? Those fierce warriors also made use of another type of blowgun. This one was shorter, a lot shorter, and designed to be inserted gently into the bottom to administer health giving coffee or cocoa enemas. We can assume the Aztecs were extremely careful not to mix up the two types of tube propped in a corner of the house, although you can imagine those vanquished people offering an enema tube to any unwelcome Spanish conquistadors who asked to try a bit of monkey hunting with a blowgun. Time to move onto the battlefield.

*****

Chapter 7
WAR STICKS

Waging war has always been one of mankind's maddest obsessions and stick technology has been at the forefront of our destructive tendencies ever since we stopped biting and clawing each other and picked something up to finish the job.

War has always been about power at some level or another and it's probably sad but true to say that a lot of the men who've ever existed have gloried in war although I'm guessing far fewer women. I'm not a warmonger but neither am I a pacifist. Did I support the Iraq War? No, I did not. Do I laud the courage and fortitude of the Allied troops who stormed the beaches of Normandy to defeat the Nazis? Yes I do.

Ever since that first hominid picked-up the first branch of a tree and used it to bash his rival our kind has had a love for the weapons we wield. Right through history men, and a lot of women too, have revered the weapons they used to maim and kill each other. You don't have to look too hard to find examples. Viking warriors gave their swords and axes blood-curdling names and so did the Ancient Britons. Who among us has not heard of King Arthur's sword Excalibur although I suspect far fewer have heard of his indomitable spear Rhongomyniad, known as Ron for short. Ron was my dad's name and trust me he speared my chest with his finger more than a few times when I'd fallen out of line. It's no different these days with modern high-tech soldiers extolling the virtues of their favourite pistol or the long-range sniper rifle they use to great effect. And just as an ancient soldier would spend hours cleaning and oiling the wood of his bow a 21st Century soldier will tend to his weapon with the same loving care

The other extraordinary thing about weapons of war is the sheer variety mankind has spawned as we adapted and fine-tuned spears and bows, swords and axes to cause the most damage in particular environments. Sticks were central to those developments, so much so that the list of clubs, spears and bows developed by man to prosecute conflict is vast and it would be impossible to list them all in a concise book such as this. In fact you could probably write a library of quite weighty textbooks about the variety of weapons developed in particular countries around the globe at particular times for particular needs.

Don't fret, that's not what I have in mind. Instead, knowing the subject to be so vast, I've set out to give you a very personal view of the forest of War Sticks by talking about some of my favourites and the stories associated with them. I've decided to begin with clubs, the decision was literally a no-brainer, then I'll discuss spears and then move on to bows and arrows. Don't forget to duck!

Imagine landing on a beach of black, volcanic pebbles with crystal blue waves lapping at the shore. Thick undergrowth fringes the beach and there's a stream nearby beckoning you to drink its cool water and so you step out of your boat. At which point your dream turns into a nightmare, as a squad of massive Polynesian warriors emerge from the undergrowth in a foul temper. It's the Eighteenth Century and it's you they're pointing their spears at, you they're bulging their eyes towards and poking their tongues at.

You can't fail to notice their weapons either. Spears, lots of spears, and knives too but quite a few of those warriors are carrying enormous, highly decorated war clubs. Trying to get a closer look at those decorations wasn't advisable but if you did you'd have seen beautiful carvings with some sort of ivory inlay and a few ivory offsets too. Actually the inlays are the teeth of men who've already been killed by that same club and the one's sticking out are sharks teeth, designed to rip your flesh. Welcome to the South Pacific, home to super warriors and a rampant culture of ritual cannibalism. Better get back into your boat before you're on the menu.

In fact Polynesian war clubs are a great example of both the sheer variety of weapons that can evolve and the respect conferred upon them by their owners and the community in general. They were and are revered by their owners and those clubs that had taken many lives were given a god-like status on the South Sea Islands of Fiji, Tonga, Samoa and Hawaii. These days they still have a high status but that's generally in the auction rooms of Europe and America where good examples of Polynesian clubs go under the hammer for a lot of money.

It has to be said the evolution of the simple club into a huge variety of types in the very confined and isolated environments of some of the South Pacific islands is truly spectacular. On Fiji alone there are about twenty or so variants, all with their own names, roughly split into two types; bludgeoning clubs and throwing clubs. My particular Fijian favourite is the totokia, which is also known as the pineapple club because of the style of carving at its head. It resembles a sort of abstract representation of the Road Runner with a sharp, almost comical beak pointing out of the head. Comical that is until you realise the beak is designed to puncture the skull of an enemy.

So let's return to that beach on a South Sea island, it happens to be Hawaii, and the man who shouldn't have got out of his boat was perhaps the greatest explorer of all time, Captain James Cook. The famous British sea captain had already mapped Newfoundland and much of the Australian coast, whilst tracking the Transit of Venus, and discovering New Zealand before going on to discover Hawaii as well. No wonder his name is honoured in bays, mountains and cities around the planet. Hawaii, however, was an island too far for Cook. At first he was greeted as a god but the shine soon wore-off and bickering between the Europeans and the Islanders developed into something more serious. It ended on the beach when Cook tried to take a local chief hostage for the return of one of his ship's cutter that had been stolen. He landed on the beach at Kealakekua Bay with a party of

Marines on 14 February 1779 and opened fire on the band of Natives.

The Englishmen were rushed by the athletic locals and overwhelmed before they had time to re-load their muskets. Cook was beaten down by war clubs, ironically while forced to use his own rifle butt as a club, then stabbed with an iron knife the natives had been given in trade by the English. What happened then is the subject of debate but there's no dispute that Cook's body was thrown into a cooking pot by King Kalaniopuu. At the time there was cannibalism on Hawaii but descendants of the King say he was honouring Cook by preparing his body in a way reserved for great men, not in order to eat him. The King kept Cook's long bones; another notable kept his scalp. Remember, this was a culture where eating the flesh of an enemy was said to imbue you with the powers that enemy had possessed in life. Cook was obviously an extraordinarily powerful spirit and we're asked to believe they didn't snack on him? Pull the other one, I say, Hawaii.

There's a paradoxical postscript to the story of Cook's great voyages of exploration in that his first vessel the Endeavour was honoured by the US space agency NASA who named a spacecraft after it. I wonder if they realised at the time that after it's heroic voyages of discovery the Endeavour had been relegated to the ignoble status of a prison hulk holding American revolutionaries in the War of Independence. It was finally scuttled, with twelve other vessels, in Narragansett Bay, Rhode Island to block the harbour entrance against French warships rushing to the aid of Washington. At the time of my writing American marine archaeologists have finally located Endeavour's watery grave and in a spirit of generous forgiveness hope to salvage some of it and restore it to its former dignity. Good luck to the Rhode Island Marine Archaeology project, I say.

As Captain Cook discovered, too late and to his dismay, clubs inflict massive injuries that forensic scientists refer to as blunt trauma and it's been happening for a long time. There's a site in Kenya where archaeologists discovered the field of a battle between warring bands of hunter-gatherers ten thousand years ago and most of the injuries were inflicted by clubs. The Roman Legions employed a club called an aklys that was held by a leather thong and in medieval times the mace was a favourite weapon of knights. It had a spiked metal head attached to the shaft and could cause a lot of damage to an enemy, particularly one on foot below the swing of a mounted, mace-wielding knight.

Native Americans especially tribes on the Great Plains, the Huron and Iroquois in the eastern forests too, used ball clubs, which are relatively free moving round, stone heads on a wooden handle. The gunstock club, which featured in the Last of the Mohicans movie, used with devastating results by that fantastic Native actor Russell Means playing Chingachgook, was popular too. It was shaped like the stock of a gun and some claim this to have been inspired by the European weapon, while others say it is a First Nation invention with a long pre-European history.

Another legendary club is the knobkerrie used to such fantastic effect on the rifle bearing British by the Zulus. Knobkerrie is the name given it by the Dutch Boer settlers while the native name is *iwisa*. It's a big piece of hardwood, usually incorporating the rootstock as the bulbous club, and decorated with ornately carved faces or sacred symbols. As a bonus it's long enough to use as a walking stick for a stroll around the veldt in times of peace.

But there was no peace during the Zulu Wars of the late Victorian era when twenty thousand Zulu warriors attacked a column of British redcoats numbering just over two thousand at Isandlwana. The odds were evened by the Brits vastly superior weapons in the form of Martini-Henry breech loading rifles but a fat lot of good the rifles turned out to be when the cartridge boxes couldn't be opened because the zinc screws holding the lids down had corroded and fused. The warriors of King Cetshwayo fell on the Brits with their assegai spears and knobkerries and slaughtered one thousand three hundred men of the column. Sadly for the Zulus it was to be a short-lived victory as the British Empire rounded on them with a vengeance. Still that battle in January 1879 ended as the worst defeat the British Army ever suffered at the hands of native warriors employing low-tech weapons. No wonder the knobkerrie features on the South African coat-of-arms.

The Irish have their own version of the knobkerrie called a shillelagh, named after a forest in County Wicklow and usually made of blackthorn. Like the knobkerrie it incorporates a root ball head and can double as a walking stick too. It's been used as a weapon on the Emerald Isle since time immemorial and I've got a nasty feeling the zealous St. Patrick would have used one to literally, rather than metaphorically, expel a few of the 'snakes' living and worshiping in Ireland. The natives of Chile have a clava, the Japanese used a Kanabo, the Australian Aboriginals a leangle or a nula-nula. Every culture had it's own club. Probably the closest, modern working relative of the club is a police officer's truncheon or nightstick and I make it my life's mission to avoid coming into contact with one of those or, indeed, the baseball bat favoured by many criminals.

These days we have clubs of a very different sort with sports clubs, drinking clubs and social clubs abounding in our culture. But the meaning has its roots in the chaos and violence of the English Civil War. Clubs began in the days when the Cavaliers and Roundheads fought a blood-soaked campaign to unseat King Charles I from his throne in favour of the

Parliamentarians led by Oliver Cromwell. Apart from the major set piece battles skirmishing and foraging parties of mounted troops from both sides of the conflict plagued the English countryside. They would charge into small towns and hamlets and make-off with whatever food and supplies they could carry. The rural communities of England became heartily sick of this untrammelled looting perpetrated by both sides in the war and came up with their own strategy. As soon as a raiding party was sighted the bells of the parish church would sound the alarm and the men and women of the village would rush back from the fields or from their workplace. Armed with their billhooks, pitchforks and cudgels they would drive the scavenging patrols away.

And they began to call themselves 'clubs' after the most common of the array of weapons they deployed against the looters and the name stuck. It became synonymous with an association of like-minded people. So we have our gentlemen's clubs, our Royal Automobile Club and of course our sporting clubs. Of these the most stick-orientated must be the Golf Club. Named after a stick, they play with a stick of the same name. So join the club everyone.

Then what about spears? A spear-carrier is, of course, the theatrical term for an extra in a stage or movie production but there was a time when the real spear-carriers were anything but relatively unimportant bit players in the production of a battle. They were the stars of the show. Spear technology has been around for at least half a million years right up to the Medieval Battles of the One Hundred Years War and even when gunpowder weapons were available skilled pike-men kept their place in the front row of a battle line-up for several generations.

But spearmen really reached their pinnacle with the Greeks and Romans when they were the cutting edge of empire building from the time of Alexander the Great when the Macedonians and Greeks under his command conquered the mighty Persian Empire. Then they established their own empire, which stretched from Egypt, where he established the city of Alexandria, to the Hindu Kush in Afghanistan and down to the Indus River in present day India. It was an astonishing three thousand miles long empire and at the heart of this extraordinary military campaign were spearmen who made-up the unassailable Macedonian Phalanx armed with relatively small shields and eighteen-foot long pikes called sarissa.

A lot of the ground work had been done by Alexander's father Phillip II who established seriously well trained regiments who worked in formations so dense even the wave of the Persian hordes broke on them when they met at the Tigris River. Alexander also developed his own Special Forces called the Hypaspists and Agrianians all experts in the use of the doru a shorter, thrusting spear. Think of it, he was just twenty-five years of age when he conquered the Persians fully three centuries before Christ was born. And we can judge just how important spears were to Alexander by his words of advice to his soldiers on maintaining military standards:

> *'How should a man be capable of grooming his own horse, or of furbishing his own spear and helmet, if he allows himself to become unaccustomed to tending even his own person, which is his most treasured belonging?'*

The Romans pretty much stole the best of Alexander's phalanx tactics and martial discipline for their world conquering Legions. Two weapons were standard and present at most of the Legion's battles; the sword called a gladius and the heavy javelin spear called a pilum. The pilum had a fairly pliable steel head that would bend on impact with an enemy shield making it extremely difficult to remove. The shield would have to be discarded leaving enemy warriors perilously exposed to the Roman advance. It was variations on these tactics that allowed the Legions to conquer the known world and on the way they gave us a word for that crushing process of conquest and it's a word related to spears.

The Romans, and indeed some of their early foes, would ritually humiliate any warriors they captured by forcing them to walk in a stooped down, bowing posture through an H-shaped frame made of three spear. It signified a loss of the vanquished warrior's manly attributes. The term they gave us comes from the Latin sub, for under, and jugum, a yolk. The word is to subjugate and so peoples were literally brought under the Roman yolk. So much for their Pax Romanum or Roman Peace, which came at the end of a spear.

Once again practically every culture has evolved it's own type of spear with Chinese and Japanese variations. The Vita was a spear developed by the Maratha regime in India and was different to most others around the world in one respect. It had a rope connecting a soldier's wrist to his spear, which meant he could retrieve his weapon after throwing it. Unsurprisingly this design didn't catch on outside the region. It might allow you to get your weapon back but if you hurt a bloke on the other side and didn't kill him he'd just have to follow the cord back to find you and get his own back. I would not be throwing a Vita at anyone, thank you very much. In Central America there was also a spear with a difference and a name like a Mexican restaurant called the tepoztopilli wielded by the fierce and feared Aztecs. It was about the height of a man with a bladed edge at the top inset with sharp-as-a- razor obsidian stone blades and designed to jab and slash. Nasty.

Later, in Europe, some equally famous spear-carriers earned their place in the pomp and ceremony of the Vatican. In the sixteenth century mercenary soldiers from Switzerland were among the most sort after in Renaissance Europe. They specialized in the use of long pikes to disrupt and disperse cavalry charges. In the early 1500's one of the Popes took them onto his books as bodyguards and in 1527 one hundred and forty seven of the Papal Swiss Guard gave their lives in a pitched battle with troops of the Holy Roman Empire, during the sack of Rome. These days the colourful Swiss Guard are seen at all the formal ceremonies at the Vatican but they carry modern firearms and train in unarmed combat. If you fancy joining and you are not a Swiss Catholic man aged between nineteen and thirty, who has already completed basic military training with the Swiss Army, forget it.

When spears are used on horseback they're known as lances and are usually longer than a spear but not as long as a pike. To survive battle lancers have to be formidably skilful exponents of their chosen profession and in the eighteenth and nineteenth centuries there were none more so than the light cavalry of America. Hats off to the Native Americans of the Great Plains, who were lancers par excellence. They honed their skills on buffalo hunts but used them to great effect in tribal wars then along came Europeans with firearms and their Stone Age culture was all but wiped out. One of the most poigniant stories of those cruelly outnumbered Native warriors is the tradition of the coup stick. Counting coup was the way young Native Braves showed how fearless they were by charging up to the enemy, usually on horseback, and striking one of them with hand, bow or a decorated coup stick. Other ways to count coups include stealing an enemy's weapons or his horses.

When the Natives of the Great Plains first encountered white settlers some of them were as good as their tradition and challenged the newcomers with coup sticks and were simply shot down out of hand. Just a tiny fragment of the outrages visited on that pristine Stone Age community by the tide of Europeans. But in World War II an extraordinary Native man called Joe Medicine Crow, who was brought up on a Crow tribal reservation in Montana, satisfied honour in the most extraordinary way by counting coup against the Nazis. He joined the U.S. Army in 1943 and was appointed a scout with the 103rd Infantry Division. Beneath his uniform he had war paint; under his helmet a yellow eagle feather.

Among his exploits Chief Medicine Crow counted coup by slapping a German without killing him, stole another Nazi's weapon, led a successful 'war party' on a raid and boldly stole fifty horses belonging to the SS singing a Crow honour song as he drove them off. He'd done enough to become a Crow War Chief and earn many gallantry awards including the highest France can offer, the Legion d' Honneur. What a splendid fellow he was but now sadly passed away into the Hunting Grounds of his gods.

In the Nineteenth Century some very different Lancers, brave men led by fools, were almost obliterated in one of the most famous Cavalry charges in history.

> *'Half a league, half a league,*
> *Half a league onward,*
> *All in the valley of Death*
> *Rode the six hundred.*
> *"Forward, the Light Brigade!*
> *Charge for the guns!" he said.*
> *Into the valley of Death*
> *Rode the six hundred.'*

It was the infamous Charge of the Light Brigade, of course, and it happened in October 1854 during the Crimean War waged between British Empire and the Russian one; pretty much at the same time as the tensions caused by the Great Game.

What happened, or more correctly who was to blame, is still the subject of some pretty futile debate. I will attempt to boil it down to a couple of sentences. The Light Brigade led by the Earl of Cardigan was sent on a mission that should have been assigned to the better armed Heavy Brigade and not only that, they were led in a charge against the wrong target. Essentially a number of woolly-headed toffs cocked the whole job up while the unflinching Lancers paid with life and limb. Not a lot of good came out of it except a better than average elegiac poem by Longfellow and an excellent, swashbuckling movie taking the rise out of said toffs.

What the poor Light Brigade had been doing was 'Tilting at Windmills' an expression that means to mistake your enemies or to pursue a vainglorious course with no chance of a successful outcome. I don't think it would have been of much comfort to those smashed up Lancers to learn the expression comes from the comical quests of a fictional Spanish lancer called Don Quixote, written by Miguel de Cervantes in the 15th Century. Tilting was the name given to jousting with a lance and our hero Don Quixote mistakes a group of windmills for giants.

His long-suffering squire Sancho Panza warns him,

> "Take care, sir. Those over there are not giants but windmills. Those things that seem to be their arms are sails which, when they are whirled around by the wind, turn the millstone."

Quixote will have none of it and the bungling Spanish knight charges and of course he's toppled from his saddle by the revolving sail of the first windmill he tilts much to Sancho's chagrin. Therein lies a lesson for us all and it took a War Stick to teach it. And with that I'll place my spear into the weapons rack and prepare to string my bow.

There are a couple of things I need to get off my chest before talking about bows and arrows. The thing of it is my partner Stephanie is a dab hand with a bow and arrow. She owns three long bows and never needs a second invitation to set up a target and shoot arrows. When she bought her first bow in a hunting store back home in the United States she asked to look at a long bow. The owner started to give her one of those 'that's a bit too much for you little lady' chats but she insisted. Okay. So he took Stephanie and the bow to the shooting range; most good hunting stores in the US have one on the premises. He gave her eight arrows and pointed to the target down range.

"You ever shot a bow before," says he.

"Sure, a little bit," says she and with that fires all eight arrows into a cluster in and around the bulls-eye.

"Yup," says the owner, "That'll do." Then asked if she wanted it gift wrapped

You see Stephanie has a strong blend of Native American in her blood. On her father's side she goes back to the great Lakota Sioux war chief Red Cloud and on her mother's she has Paiute ancestry from the desert tribe of Death Valley in Nevada. But there's more. When her father looked into the European family tree for both his side and her mother's, incredibly he found that both lines wound back across the Atlantic to South West Wales where my own family roots lie and where I was born.
Coincidence? I'm not so sure. Meant to be? Of course, and what's more it has a great deal to do with War Sticks because bow technology is at the heart of her heritage. Stephanie's Native ancestors relied totally on their stick culture and a bow

112

and arrow was never far from their hands. And don't forget the Welsh who were lauded too for their skills with the long bow giving good service as mercenaries unleashing a 'rain of death' for English kings at battles like Crecy and Agincourt. Little wonder she's a natural with DNA like that.

I'm okay with a bow myself but confess I play 'second string' to Stephanie, as the saying goes, when it comes to firing arrows at targets. No self-respecting archer would take to the field without a 'second string' in case the first, usually the best one, snapped and the other expression 'more strings to my bow' comes from that same root. The truth is if I were around at the time of those medieval wars I might have been practicing with a bow until my fingers bled. Why? Just think of the terrible close quarter gore of hand-to-hand fighting with clubs, spears and swords. Surely it would have been much better to be well behind the front line launching the dreaded 'arrow storm' onto the enemy? Better by far to chill with your mates in between letting fly a few arrows when your commander gave the word safe in the knowledge arrows are a lot faster and travel a lot further than spears. There's nothing like putting a bit of distance between yourself and danger, right? A bit like being in the modern artillery miles behind the lines firing volleys of high explosive into the enemy.

Well not quite, even though artillery was originally the name given to the line of archers. The truth is archers were too close to the thick of it to avoid getting embroiled in the blood and guts although they did have some perks. It's recorded that Welsh archers at Crecy would make a few shillings by rushing onto any fallen enemy knights and hamstringing them with a knife so that they couldn't escape the battlefield. When it was all over the poor knights who'd suffered the fate of Achilles would be ransomed and the ever-pragmatic archers would get a tip from their own nobles.

Bows have been around for a long time and, just like their stick cousins the club and the spear, they come in a dizzying variety of types all around our planet. Wood isn't always the best archaeological source but there are arrowheads dating back sixty thousand years from the same hunter-gatherer battlefield in South Africa as those club wounds I mentioned. In Germany there are fragments of bows dating back eighteen thousand years and there's evidence of them in every culture since. Bows and arrows were the ancient version of the cruise missile, a delivery system so fast and far-reaching in their time they attracted great reverence and significant gods in many religions are all depicted carrying bows. And that's the characteristic that elevates the bow above other stick weapons, however much they are revered. Diana, the huntress, Artemis the moon goddess too and then there's Cupid, a construct of the Roman god Amor and the Greek Eros; never forget Cupid whose arrows of love have brought down billions of humans.

There are so many Gods and Goddesses in so many ancient cultures depicted carrying a bow. The Sumerian Enlil, the Norse god Hoor, who's tricked into killing his brother with an arrow made of mistletoe, and then there's the Hindu god Rama who's an archer too. And the reason for this plethora of archer deities lies in the night sky where the constellation of Orion's Belt sparkles in the shape of a bow ready to be pulled to shoot a star across the heavens. Neither does this reverence end in the distant past with the fading memory of ancient gods. Orion still pulls on mankind's fascination with the bow and arrow so that it endures, even defying the tide of digital technology. Just think how many video games involve bows and what about their continued representation in popular culture in movies like The Hunger Games. How many girls in their teens dreamt of Legolas when the Lord of the Rings movies came onto our screens or boys beguiled by Zena the Warrior Princess? Quite simply bows rock.

In the UK there's wonderful evidence of a special bowman who, coincidentally, hailed from the same area of the European Alps as our friend Otzi the Iceman. But this archer's body wasn't tossed aside after being summarily killed. Instead he was laid to rest in an opulent burial; one of the finest from Bronze Age Britain. This man was about the same age as Otzi and surprisingly, given that his DNA showed he hailed from the same Alpine area, he was buried just three miles from Stonehenge.

His grave goods were rich and included gold hair decorations but it's the two sandstone wrist guards, to protect him from the whipping of a bow-string, and a collection of flint arrowheads that gave him his name; the Amesbury Archer. Also laid in his grave was an object called a 'cushion stone' a sort of stone pad used to work gold and bronze against. It marked him out as a metal worker and in those times that would make him a very special person indeed.

What we know of his life as told from the grave shows us quite clearly that bowmen travelled, in his case from the Alps to the remote island of Britain, a distance of some twelve hundred miles. There's long been a tendency in our car driving society to imagine ancient people lived their lives attached to one particular landscape, confined to three of four local villages with an occasional trip to the nearest market or festival. In fact many of those prehistoric folk were great adventurers and travelled widely. I'm sure the Amesbury Archer came along well trodden paths across Europe then crossed to Britain on a regular cross channel ferry service probably at the narrowest point of the sea between Boulogne and Dover where there's still a ferry service run by huge car and truck transporter ships. But what evidence is there to say there was one in the Bronze Age? Well there's the Dover Boat, a Bronze Age wonder that was found during construction work in the seaport and has pride of place in the Dover Museum. It was probably about forty feet long and for propulsion had a sail and stick power in the form of oars manned by the crew; easily capable of crossing the channel. I'll be telling you more about the Dover Boat later.

After Robin Hood the Amesbury Archer is Britain's most famous bowman but who was Robin Hood? There's absolutely no historical evidence at all that he existed, no documents, no warrants from the Sheriff of Nottingham for his arrest, nothing but a 'will o' the wisp' legend. Was Robin a real life hero of the people pushing back against Norman rule, saving the oppressed Saxons who'd been overtaxed by the evil Sheriff? Or was he simply the fragment of a collective imagination, not someone who existed but someone the Saxon folk longed to exist. I think that's indeed who Robin was. A character the people longed to emerge from their midst, the one who'd right their wrongs, a romantic focus for their inner furies. Robin Hood was the hero they wanted to come along and bash their Norman bullies.

There were other mythical archers not least the famed and feared women warriors they called the Amazons who dominated the Scythian Plains of old. Supposedly they were man-haters so fierce it was said they volunteered for the mastectomy of one breast so they could fire their bows unimpeded by a voluptuous bosom. The Amazons' modus operandi was to ride into battle firing arrows as they galloped into the fray; apparently the ancient world's gay women on steroids. At one time it seemed the Ancient Greeks could speak of little else and of course in their stories all the Amazons were beautiful. In Athens it was Amazon this and Amazon that. They were the Spice Girls of Grecian popular culture.

Then time curled its mists around the Amazons and they vanished in all but name and legend until the 21st Century when archaeologists started uncovering the graves of warrior women all over the area of ancient Scythia; stretching from the Black Sea to Mongolia. They were buried with their well-fitted armour and with an array of splendid weaponry including fine bows. Most were buried with their horses too and some had the remains of their children buried with them. I've read some commentators who take this as a sign they couldn't have been the man haters depicted. How could they have had families if they hated men it's argued? There's actually no evidence either way although it's clear from the grave remains they weren't chopping their boobs off to improve their aim. If I were to speculate I'd guess the Amazons probably had more in common with Celtic women like Boudicca who fought alongside the men of their clan and certainly the Amazons must have been treated as equals too from the splendour of their burials.

It comes as no surprise to me the ancient domain of Scythia was bounded on one side by the valley of the River Don, home to the Cossacks who are some of the fiercest cavalry known to the world. And on the region's Eastern side lie the grass plains of Mongolia home to Genghis Khan's equally fierce Horde; essentially a vast army of horseback archers. With this superb military machine at his command the Khan went on to conquer an empire as impressive as that of Alexander the Great; rivalling that of Rome too. At any rate I'm prepared to bet my shirt the Cossacks and the Mongols will both have their mitochondrial rootstocks in the DNA of the Amazons.

There are so many stories of bows in battle down through the ages it's difficult to choose one from another but there is an account of one man's use of a bow that frankly amazes me simply because he pitted it against the mighty Nazi blitzkrieg. It is in fact the story of the last recorded kill by a long bow in battle and the man responsible was a British officer called Lt. Colonel Jack Churchill. At least that was his given name. The soldiers of the British Army, recognizing his fuse box was wired so completely differently to most people, called him 'Mad Jack" Churchill but never to his face.

I'll just say it in plain language and let it sink in. Mad Jack went to war against Panzer tanks and Mauser machine guns armed with a long bow, a giant Scots sword called a Claymore and a set of bagpipes. In May 1940 he led his men into an ambush on German troops in the Pas de Calais and kicked off the action by killing one of the enemy with a well-aimed arrow. His men used the more prosaic rifles they'd been issued with to kill the rest. Jack was eventually evacuated from the beaches of Dunkirk when the Nazis routed the joint French and British force and then joined the Commandoes. In 1941 he led a Commando raid on Norway playing his pipes before charging into the thick of it with a grenade and his Claymore; a weapon Bonnie Prince Charlie and Rob Roy would have been completely familiar with. Collecting gallantry medals on his way Colonel Churchill then led his Commandoes into Salerno, Italy where he and a Corporal captured forty-two Germans in the town of Molina at sword point. Later he went back into the town to retrieve his Claymore, which he'd lost in hand to hand fighting with the Nazis.

In 1944 Churchill was captured whilst fighting with Yugoslav partisans and, perhaps because of his significant surname, he was taken to Berlin before they transferred him to Sachsenhausen concentration camp. Mad Jack escaped and eventually made it to Verona in Italy where he found an American armoured unit who took him in. What a man and that long bow shot in the Pas de Calais puts him in the history books. But just how mad was Mad Jack? I'd say completely bonkers because despite the Pipes, which he played well, and the Claymore, Jack Churchill was no latter day Braveheart at all. He didn't have a single drop of Scots blood in him but I dare say he'd have got on really well with Chief Medicine Crow.

There are other sticks used in war, which can't be categorized as clubs, spears or bows but have played vital, sometimes pivotal roles in warfare. One of them is the Bangalore Torpedo. This simple device was dreamt up by a British officer serving in India; hence its name. Originally it comprised short sections of bamboo, about five feet long, that could be screwed together to make a much longer rod. At its head was an explosive charge packed into the hollow bamboo tube. It was ideal for disposing of unexploded ordnance or blowing up obstacles like coiled, barbed wire defences. The U.S. Army adopted them and designated them as the M1A1 Bangalore Torpedo and the weapon came into its own on the coast of Normandy on D-Day. US troops were pinned down on Omaha Beach and being cut to pieces by withering German fire when a Colonel decided it was time to deploy the torpedoes. They were used to blow through barbed wire entanglements and eventually to undermine a concrete bunker housing lethal machine guns. This gave the hard-pressed Americans the route off the beach they so badly needed and it's depicted in a scene from that great movie The Longest Day with Robert Mitchum chewing on a cigar as Bangalore Torpedoes saved the day.

Another War Stick that simply can't be ignored carries the focus of fervour for fighting men and women. It's the flag. Flags have been around for a very long time and one found in modern Iran, made of a bronze sheet fixed to a pole, dates back four and a half thousand years. The Chinese and Indians were the first to use them commonly in battle and eventually they came to be used as national standards until these days reverence of national flags seems to have become hard wired into our psyches as they fulfil some deep seated need for symbolism in our lives. And of course without a stick to hang it from the flag would be a sad, drooping sort of dishcloth.

With its stick it becomes a snapping emblem full of vim and vigour; something worth following if necessary until death.

At my partner Stephanie's home in Massachusetts we fly the US flag, the fabulous Stars and Stripes, and below it a slightly smaller Welsh flag, the glorious Red Dragon. In Welsh it's called Y Ddraig Goch and it's obviously the most vivid and dramatic standard on the planet and that's me being completely objective. It was indeed the flag that Henry VII had at the head of his army when he defeated the crooked backed King Richard III at the Battle of Bosworth and it symbolized Henry's Tudor's Welsh roots. Richard himself in his final, unsuccessful and totally courageous last rush of arms killed Henry's standard-bearer Sir William Brandon, graphically demonstrating the level of significance attached to the flag as a rallying point. If the Standard falls then what do the men have to follow? They may assume their side has lost and void the field of battle and so protection of the Standard has become something of a military cult.

This reached its zenith on the depressingly bloody battlefields of the American Civil War where men on either side would go to extraordinary lengths to protect their regimental Color. It's said that no fewer than eight men from the legendary New York Irish Brigade were killed or wounded carrying their flag at Antietam in 1862. A year later at the Battle of Gettysburg unionist soldiers of the 16th Maine were surrounded so they tore their regimental Color into strips and each man hid a piece in their own clothing when they were captured. Those pieces that returned with the men at the end of the war became part of Maine's culture and the State's colourful story. To this day the U.S. military give the role of Color Guard an extremely high status.

There's one other War Stick I must tell you about as it sums up the resilience and quiet fortitude of Britain during World War

II. It's June 1940. By some miracle we'd managed to rescue most of our army from the beaches of Dunkirk and after sizing us up for a few months Hitler has started a campaign to bomb our island into submission. The Battle of Britain had begun. Our backs were to the wall. Our American friends had not yet entered the fray and we were all that lay between Hitler and the rest of the world and all that stood between certain invasion and us were the Spitfire and Hurricane fighter planes and their indomitable pilots.

My Uncle Cliff was one of them. He flew a Hurricane and broke his back in a crash landing somewhere in Southern England during those frantic dogfight days. I never heard Uncle Cliff talk about his experiences but ever after he sported his RAF fighter pilot's moustache. He was one of The Few as Churchill called those pilots who sometimes scrambled four or five times a day to fight against odds usually set at five to one. And there were sticks that literally plotted every raid, every repulse of enemy formations, every attack by our squadrons and every plane that was downed on either side. They resembled a croupier's rake, you know the ones they use in casinos to shove the chips onto the bets, and they were used with great skill by members of the Women's Auxiliary Air Force on the huge map mounted on the flat plotting table in the Operations Room.

There'd be four of five WAFS, as they were lovingly called, around the table with the Ops Room commanders watching and instructing from a gallery above as they moved numbered, wooden checkers around the board to represent Luftwaffe groups coming in to the attack and our chaps going up to meet them. All the while the radio exchanges with our squadrons could be heard on loudspeakers around the room and sometimes they'd listen in real time to one of our own being shot down. What stoic and fantastically courageous people they were.

At first the Nazis concentrated their attacks on shipping in the English Channel, then they moved to attack our fighter bases and the WAFS found themselves plotting Luftwaffe formations coming straight at them. Fighter stations were bombed and Ops Rooms were hit, showering the plotting table with debris. No problem. They simply moved the whole kitting caboodle to the local pub and during this dramatic time five of those wonderful WAFS were given gallantry medals for refusing to abandon their posts during attacks.

On August 20th 1940 Winston Churchill visited the main Ops Room in a bunker at Uxbridge, West London. It was at the height of the Nazi attacks and as he was about to step into his car at the end of a torrid three hours he told his aides, "Do not speak to me. I have never been so moved." And as they drove in silence back to Westminster he came up with the unforgettable phrase he was to deliver in Parliament a few days later, "Never in the field of human conflict was so much owed, by so many, to so few."

Churchill returned to the Uxbridge bunker in September when the Luftwaffe, infuriated by their inability to bring the RAF to its knees, threw everything they had at Britain in an airborne frenzy. They failed and with their losses running unacceptably high the Nazis abandoned their raids and their planned invasion of Britain, code named Operation Sea Lion. The WAFS plotting sticks, which had played a seemingly small but absolutely vital role in Britain's hour of greatest danger, were left to rest on the plotting table. Those women had truly been the croupiers of the war placing high stakes wagers against the Nazis backing Britain's future. I hope the generations to come will not forget them.

Chapter 8
GOOD STICKS

Sticks are of course inert objects and it is we humans who decide the uses they are put too for good or evil. We've already seen a great deal of stick usage for power totems, implements of war and to exact cruel punishment. That's down to us. The Stick has no choice. But I'd like to think that if you were to weigh Good Sticks in the scale against their uses for evil there would be plenty to redress the balance and so I'm going to discuss the sticks that sustained us in so many ways.

In truth but for sticks I'd not be writing this book at all. It was five thousand years ago that an ancient king of Mesopotamia is credited with first using writing on a tablet of clay making simple marks with reeds sticks. Those first inscriptions were records of transactions but soon phonetics left the cuneiform alphabets behind and written language became a thrilling explosion of description and narrative. It moved from tablets of clay and wax onto paper, then printing presses were invented until these days we live in a world where trillions of words fill the boundless ether.

In our earliest days as a species we harnessed sticks to provide us with the warmth of the fire and then to cook our food and, twisted into simple torches, to light our way through the dark. At certain times in our development we chose to inhabit caves wherever we could find them. Who knows what global climatic or geological event had forced that choice upon us or whether it was simply for security from the big beasts roaming outside. But when we came out into the light again it was sticks that gave us the frames for our tents and our simple houses. So it was that sticks provided us with those basic needs and as we marched on down the millennia they continued to give us those sustainable, forest born benefits. For many communities across the planet in jungles, on vast grassland plains and in the frozen wastes of the Arctic Circle they continue to do so to this day despite the relative rarity of trees in some of those habitats.

There are three or four stick-reliant dwellings that come to mind immediately and they are all of ancient provenance. The first is the Tipi, the iconic home of the Plains Natives of North

America; tribes like the Lakota, the Ogallala, the Crow and others. A framework of poles covered with buffalo hides kept those indigenous people safe from the elements on Plains which are burning hot in summer, freezing in winter and endlessly windy. The Tipi was also portable and allowed the tribe to respond rapidly to the movements of the huge bison herds they followed and relied on for their survival. They simply packed everything up and loaded it onto a 'skid' or travois made from a couple of the poles, which were dragged along by horses or dogs from one encampment to the next. Tipis are not to be confused with wigwams or wikiups, which are dome-shaped, covered in bark and more permanent homes. Oh, the versatility of sticks!

A world away on the steppes of Mongolia the clans came up with a parallel but different housing solution for their lives as nomadic herdsmen. It's called the Yurt or Ger and once again poles form the framework, although this time covered in a dense felt made from sheep and goat wool that shrugged off the plentiful snow and the rare rainstorms that fell on those infinite grasslands. The only problem with Yurts is the almost complete lack of timber out on the Steppes and so the original Mongolians, just like the modern ones, had to trade for wood from other regions. Despite the shortage of wood Yurts have been used on the Steppes of Asia for around three thousand years and were first described by the classic Greek historian Herodotus as the dwellings of the Scythians, that horse riding, bow firing nation that ruled the region for nearly a thousand years. That's right the same Scythians who boasted some of the fiercest women warriors the world has ever known among their ranks and so we can say with some confidence that Yurts were the Palaces of the Amazons.

In recent times Yurts and Tipis have been marketed commercially and 'brought up to date' by western copycats but in Mongolia at least the originals are still the fundamental basis for a continuing culture and long may it be so. The same goes for the wandering Sami reindeer herders of the Scandinavian Arctic from Norway across Finland and into northern Sweden. The shelter they use as they follow the herds across the snow-draped tundra is the Lavvu. It's very similar to the American Tipi except its outline is squatter on the horizon making it more windproof. Incredibly the Lavvu needs not a single guy rope or stake in the ground to hold it down. It seems the ancient Sami architects had flat-pack minds and built stability into their design.

During World War II the Sami lands were at the heart of a frozen battlefield between the Nazis and the Russians as the local indigenous people looked on unable to help themselves. The Russians systematically burnt out the permanent villages where the Sami lived between reindeer migrations. It was the Lavvu that saved their lives as lodge poles came to the rescue and they were able to flee into the wilderness and cling onto life. Little wonder the humble Lavvu became a potent totem for the Sami and a rallying symbol for Sami self-determination. These days they have their own Parliament, the Samediggi, at Karasjok in the Finnmark region of Norway and its design, in glass and wood, reflects the shape of the life-giving Lavvu

Nowadays modern Tipis, Yurts or Lavvu will accommodate small wood burning stoves with a chimney for heat and cooking but originally they would have had open fires, either in a pit lined with grass or moss or set on a slab of stone directly below the chimney flap. By using the right wood and tending the fire carefully they could keep their tents smoke free and safe. But my next classic, stick-built home, the Celtic roundhouse, could not have accommodated a chimney on grounds of health and safety. It's height and the optimal angle of construction of around forty-five degrees would have ensured a strong draft and vortex of heat that would have set the thatch ablaze at the chimney hole. Instead they let the smoke gather in the lintels and filter slowly through the thatch, spreading the heat and depositing tar as an extra layer of waterproofing. They knew what they were doing those folk. Round houses were pretty much ubiquitous in Bronze Age and Iron Age Britain, sometimes built on stilts or platforms over lakes, connected to the land by a gangplank for extra security. I really fancy living in one of those Crannochs as they're called and sometimes dream of re-building one found by archaeologists on Llangorse Lake in the Welsh mountains near the town of Brecon. Sadly I'd have to employ bows and arrows, spears and other stick weapons to drive off the rest of the tourists who enjoy the lake these days so I just keep on dreaming.

All over our planet sticks have been used in a quite mind-boggling array of houses of different kinds, employing different approaches to various problems, but one technique that crossed from the Iron Age to the Medieval and indeed to the present is known as wattle and daub. The wattle is a cross-weave of strips of sticks, usually hazel or willow, to create a panel. The panel is then placed in the framework of a wall, usually timber, and the daub is added. Depending on the era that could be mud mixed with cow manure or a lime plaster but it's all slapped on the wattle panel and skimmed off to a reasonably smooth surface before it's allowed to dry.

The idea probably came from the wattle panels made to fence in sheep at shearing time and the supply of sticks to make these hurdles, as they're called, depends on the ancient woodland craft of coppicing. Coppicing relies on the fact that some species of tree, including hazel, willow, oak and birch, will throw out new growth after their branches have been cut right back to the trunk and sometimes down almost to the ground. This new growth will shoot up quickly and will be reasonably straight as it races towards the light. It can then be harvested in bundles or faggots for a number of uses, including wattle, hurdles or charcoal. Coppicing is finger trapping, all weather work. It's not for the idle or faint hearted. It's also a fantastically sustainable way of managing woodland and like many of the subjects I mention in this book, merits an entire volume of its own. In these days of super fast tree felling machines a lot of woodland is harvested rather than coppiced and original, coppiced woodland is a rare thing indeed.

So are the chalk streams of England, one of the rarest habitats in the world, and nowadays sticks play a crucial role in their management. These streams rise in the chalk hills of Southern England and are fed by springs where water that has soaked into the permeable chalk bursts when the pressure is great enough. Chalk streams are wide and shallow with gin clear water running over gravel beds and in summer the surface of the stream is carpeted with the white flowers of ranunculus; the water daisy. There are precisely two hundred and ten such streams in the world and one hundred and sixty of them are in England, the rest in the Pas de Calais in Northern France, and they are the focus some of the most sought after wild trout fishing in the world.

I am blessed to live in a cottage on the banks of a chalk stream and from a garden seat I can sit and watch the river and nature meander past me. Quite often it's considerably faster than a meander as the sapphire jewel of the kingfisher darts downstream with a thin whistle. A myriad insects from moths to dragonflies feed the Daubenton's water bats at dusk and the water vole, famous Ratty from Wind in the Willows, often swims by. Ratty is the UK's most threatened mammal and the chalk streams where they like to make a home are among our most threatened of habitats because millions of gallons of water are drawn out of the chalk hills to supply big towns and cities. This abstraction depletes the flow of the streams, which in turn inhibits the growth of the ranunculus weed and the river life that depends on it.

Not a good situation overall but what has this got to do with sticks you might ask? Cast your minds back to the start of this book when I introduced you to a character called John Hounslow. He's the one who tried to assassinate my son Harry and I with a killer boomerang cleverly disguised as a holiday gift. Well, John is a River Keeper tending to the delicate environment of our local chalk stream the River Kennet and his pivotal role is to work with the fishing club, environmental groups and government agencies to maintain the balance of the river as best they can. The fact of the matter is that sucking off millions of gallons of water for peoples' taps badly affects the flow and there's a knock on effect in the growth of the water daisy which is the foundation of the eco system. Poor flow equals poor river, equals stressed wildlife. Time to call in the coppicer. And that's just what John does to help narrow the stream at key spots on its length and hence increase the flow to keep the habitat happy.

John gives his coppicing associate Deane Gregory a call and then Deane goes out into the woodland he tends somewhere in the neighbouring county of Hampshire. He cuts bundles of hazel faggots about ten feet long and a couple of armfuls wide and delivers them to the riverbank. John then drives a double line of posts into the riverbed to hold the bundles securely in place. Anchored in this way they create a new, artificial bank and later on John back-fills the space behind with soil to narrow the course of the river and speed up the flow. It doesn't take long for vegetation to bind the whole thing in so naturally that the untutored eye would never know what the River Keeper had created. It's heart warming to see the results as the wildlife of the valley is sustained. Wild trout rise for the mayfly and at night I hear otters whistling to each other as

129

water bats dip to feed in the mirror above the trout. All because John has sped the flow to make the water daisy grow.

Sticks then have given us warmth and shelter down the ages and here they are in an ancient form, re-invented to help us protect a precious habitat against the enormous pressures that ever-growing urban populations place on the countryside. Useful sticks, good sticks indeed. And if any of you doubt the durability of sticks in construction then travel to Asia, Africa or South America where they're still utilised, not least in countries like India and China, where vast towers of scaffolding made of bamboo are an everyday sight on construction sites.

There are other Good Sticks of course and when mankind was making the transition form hunter-gatherer to settled farmer about twelve thousand years ago sticks played a vital role in early agriculture and some of those implements, one in particular, is still in use around the globe. A lot of people including my mother, when she was still alive, call it a dibber. Anthropologists and their ilk prefer to call it a Planting Stick and it is probably the first agricultural tool that mankind used as soon as we realised that if you got seeds under the ground in a particular area then you could watch them grow and eventually harvest them. Step one was to get the seed into the soil and the simplest method is to poke a hole with a stick, drop the seed in and cover it over. Hence the Planting Stick and lots of people that 'garden' crops like peas, beans, marrows still use a dibber of one sort or another. That's certainly the case in modern Mexico where every home with a garden has a version of the Aztec Digging Stick called the Uictli that was used to create a tilth as well as for the planting of seeds.

Growing crops like that on a farm scale is labour intensive but people had no television and hunger is a hard taskmaster so the work had to be done. While the crops were growing they had to be protected from weeds that might smother them and pests that wanted to eat them. In the case of grain harvests that would generally be birds and so people took sticks and made catapults out of them to drive the flocks away and, with a bit of luck, eat a few in the process. When it came to harvesting the first scythes were made of sticks with flints inserted along the length to create a cutting edge. In ancient Britain examples of rakes made from antlers tied to Sticks have been found and the earliest ploughs or awls were made of a solid wooden upright with a sharp stick slotted through the end to cut through the surface of the soil.

The point is that these ancient prototypes sowed the seeds of ideas that are still incorporated in most of the sophisticated, digitally guided farm machinery we see on the land today; a legacy of the Stick Age. With the harvest gathered our forebears could eat, which might seem quite obvious in today's world but was a lot less certain in times past. Harvests failed and famine hobbled across the land. When the harvest was good though we used sticks to help us eat. We carved spoons from them to stir and eat the food we cooked and in Far Eastern cultures chopsticks are the accepted way of devouring rice-based dishes.

Spits for roasting meat over an open fire were originally sticks then metal took their place and we used sticks for baking too. Stephanie's mother Diana and her dad Rex Shelburne used to buy and sell antiques when they lived in the town of Ogallala, Nebraska in the Mid-West of America. Before my British friends scoff at the prospect of American antiques as compared to the wealth of historic items here in the UK let me defend the American legacy. There are some really fascinating items connected with the indigenous tribes and then the first colonisation of the Eastern seaboard, the War of Independence and the Civil War.

But my favourites are those linked to that massive and controversial human project; the colonisation of the Wild West. It's hard to escape some knowledge of it if only through the refracting prism of Hollywood 'westerns' however where John Wayne went we will follow. Enter the pie stick or pie lifter owned by the Shelburne's. It's a split stick with two rectangles of wire protruding from the end forming two letter P's back to back. By twisting the stick the wire P's flip together and can be used to grip hot pies or bread and snatch them from an oven. The pie stick would have been found resting alongside the small, cast iron oven that sat on the tail of a chuck wagon. That was the mobile kitchen at the heart of every wagon train carrying Europe's 'huddled masses yearning to breathe free' in their relentless journey across America in search of land, gold or quite often anonymity. The oven would often be kept burning low throughout the day literally baking pies as they traversed the Great Plains and the Rockies. The weak and the sick might take some relief from its heat as the bone cutting winds of the Plains chased them. What a story and the humble pie stick played a vital role in one of the greatest human migrations of modern history.

There are lots of sticks in the world of cuisine from kebab sticks to cocktail sticks and I'm reminded of a situation where using a specific stick for the wrong purpose was fated to fail. It's the story of a cocktail stick and a scientific experiment. While I went into journalism my younger brother Gareth had a natural bent towards a career in science. After studying marine biology he went on to become a Professor of Environmental Science, a world authority on water quality and a special advisor to Parliamentary Select Committees, the World Health Organisation and the U. S. Environmental Protection Agency no less. Along his career journey he also fulfilled a childhood vow to clean the sewage from the seas off Wales, where we were raised, doing so as an advisor to a water company's update of their coastal outfalls. Gareth died of cancer in 2008. I was enormously proud of him; still am. But one of his achievements truly demonstrated the ubiquitous nature of our relationship with sticks. He was still a young research graduate when he telephoned me to tell me about a scientific breakthrough he'd made. He was cock-a-hoop. "I'm in this week's New Scientist, Al!"

"Are you? What for?"

"Well there's this tiny annelid that lives at the very end of the spiral in a hermit crab's shell."

"What's an annelid?" I interrupted.

"A worm. It's a tiny sea worm and it comes out of it's hiding place to feed on the left overs from the crab's meals. Thing is no one's been able to get an entire live specimen out of the top of the spiral shell but I've done it. I got one."

"Why hadn't anyone else done it before?" I asked.

"Well people saw the tip off the shell but the worm is so small and tucked in so tight everyone's been trying to winkle it out with needles. I've even tried with cocktail sticks but every time the poor worm gets crushed or cut in two."

"So how did you manage to do it?"

"Guinness. I put a couple of drops of Guinness into the tank with a pipette and the worm just got drunk and rolled out of its own accord. Brilliant, even if I say so myself."

The thing about Gareth was he had a very well honed sense of humour and even though it wasn't April Fools Day I was sceptical, "Pull the other one! Why didn't you use a couple of drops of Martini instead then you could have given your annelid an olive on the cocktail stick."

"You can take the mickey if you want Al but you won't be so clever when you've read the New Scientist. And anyway all I had in the fridge was a bottle of Guinness."
He was right and I had to eat my words after reading the piece. It was true my brilliant younger brother had made a small contribution to scientific history simply by substituting Guinness for a failed cocktail stick.

For two weekends in the autumn each year the high street of the ancient Borough of Marlborough is closed to traffic as the annual Mop Fair takes over the town. These days it's a flashing whirligig of fairground rides but once upon a time it was an entirely different affair and the clue is in the name. A mop of course is a cloth on the end of a stick used to clean floors and the Mop Fair came about as a hiring fair in the medieval and it coincided with that important time of the agricultural year called harvest home; when all is safely gathered in from the fields.

House servants and farm labourers would be looking for a change of boss and they would head for the fair carrying the tools of their trade. In the case of a housemaid it would be her mop, a farmworker would turn up with his scythe or pitchfork and so on. There'd be games and food stalls and jugglers and importantly prospective employers who would promenade the high street interviewing workers on the hoof, so to speak. There are no work opportunities at the Mop Fair these days and there haven't been for a long time, unless of course you're a fairground worker, but I thought I would metaphorically mop-up some of the Good Stick stories that haven't fitted with ease into the previous chapters or the one to come. Perhaps I should start with the obvious; the walking stick.

I've already talked about my own love of a good stick but before I say a little bit more about walking sticks let me get one set out of the way and never mention them again. I'm talking about Nordic Poles; you know those aluminium ski-style poles that have usurped the traditional wooden prototype. I am not a fan of the Nordic Pole. Okay, they're supposed to be fitness aids, for the ambulatory elderly in particular, but for the life of me I can't understand why people should want to do simulated cross country skiing across the fundamentally snow free British countryside. Those poles are expensive and in my view they're entirely impractical. Try knocking down a clump of nettles overhanging a path with one of those aluminium pseudo sticks; it's likely to buckle. Not for me a Nordic Pole. Not ever.

Walking sticks come in all shapes and sizes of course and in different cultures they are accorded differing levels of significance. There was a time when no self-respecting Dandy would be seen in London society without a silver topped stick, often with a sword blade operated by a switch secreted in the end. Swagger sticks are the ones army officers carry under their arms and use to poke around the barracks looking for faults. Thumb sticks and shepherds crooks, on the other hand, seem to flock together most commonly, with their owners, at country shows in the UK these days but the art of Stick Dressing is alive and well with craftsmen carving everything from a pheasant's head to a bone whistle for a handle and classes in the art are held all over the country.

I have a couple of friends who can eye-up a hazel hedge when the leaf has fallen in autumn and pick a perfect stick. One of them is a farmer pal called John Kerr, the other a photographer I work with from time to time, called Les Wilson. They unerringly reach their hand in to grasp a straight hazel stick, which forks into two at its top, cut it and dress it with a knife into a thumb-stick that fits their hand perfectly. I confess I find it slightly annoying as frankly I'm not so good at stick dressing and prefer to buy my sticks ready dressed from Jean Upton's treasure trove of a country shop just off Marlborough High Street.

Then there's basket weaving. The ancient Mesopotamians believed that baskets are the children of the Gods who wove a wickerwork raft, floated it on the oceans then covered it in soil to create the land. Basket making was one of our first technologies, created by the sheer necessity of having to get the gathered harvest from the forest or joints of flesh from the kill back to the village. Indeed the oldest baskets identified by science are around twelve thousand years old but they must certainly go back much further. It also means that baskets pre-date pottery and indeed probably inspired pottery and they were certainly used to fire the first pots, which bear the imprints of basketry inside. Why? Because the ancients packed clay around a basket then fired it. The clay baked hard into a pot while the woven sticks inside burnt away. There's nothing new about human ingenuity.

Native Americans were among the many cultural groups who achieved great beauty with their colourful woven baskets and to this day wicker furniture is much admired around the globe. In a corner of my bedroom I have an example. It's a small wicker armchair that belonged to my grandmother. A simple linear pattern was sprayed in paint on it before it was sold. It is a piece of wartime Utility furniture, created to save wood and metal for the war effort against the Nazis and so I treasure it for the history of sacrifice for the greater good it represents.

Where would we be without these Good Sticks? Around the time that baskets were being complemented by pottery for carriage and storage people were starting to weave. We'd already finely honed our sewing techniques using bone needles to stitch deerskins and fur into durable clothing or moccasin-style footwear. But we were growing wool on the flocks of sheep and goats our developing pastoral society depended upon. So it was that woven textiles were hit upon to transform warm and workable wool into clothing. But without one simple stick weaving would not have been possible. It's called a shuttle and it is passed back and forth to create the weft and weave of cloth.

There are many Good Sticks in culture too. It's a coincidence that the American publisher of this volume is called Talking Stick Books. In Native American culture a stick is dressed with feathers and beads and is held by the person talking in tribal counsels or telling some ancient saga around the campfire. Importantly the presence of the Talking Stick means those not holding the stick must hold their tongues instead. That's a Good Stick indeed.

So too are the sticks represented on the cover of this book painted by my hugely talented collaborator Alex Merry who created the illustrations on these pages. Alex comes from a family of talented artists. Her sister Kate is a fine painter too; more of Kate later. But Alex has another persona and is wont to transform| herself into an edgy performer with wild make-up and crazy costumes as one of a very modern Morris Dancing troupe called Boss Morris, based in the Cotswold town of Stroud. The sticks on the cover of this book are their Morris Dancing Sticks. Without them the dance would not be complete and I love them.

My youngest son Morgan is also a talented fellow with a particular handle on good sticks. He's a traditional blacksmith who creates beautiful artefacts from the fire of the forge with an anvil and a hammer. Morgan studied for three years at the National School of Blacksmithing near the City of Hereford under the tutelage of two fantastic teachers; Chris Blythman and Pete Smith. The creation of hand wrought metalwork is, of course, a cultural thing and is deeply ingrained in our species history as magical and spiritual so that the anvil and the hammer are the tools of the gods in many cultures. Thor's hammer was fundamental to the beliefs of the Vikings, the Celts held Brigit divine as the goddess of hearth and forge and the Saxons had the mischievous Wayland the Smith. Further afield the Hindus of India and the Yoruba tribe of Nigeria all hold their blacksmith gods sacred and a lot of young, modern blacksmiths I've met truly believe the Gods of the forge are real.

I never had the opportunity to watch Morgan work metal during the years of his studies. I saw the results but I'd never watched him at the anvil. Then one day at his friend Tom Southerden's forge at Buscot on the banks of the upper reaches of the River Thames I watched my son heat and strike and quench the metal and strike again with his favourite hammer; one with a hickory handle. And there's the stick in this story as one thing's for certain a blacksmith's hammer won't strike without the stick they call a handle. Unyielding metal will never do, as it would send a shock through the Smith's hand that would reverberate down to his very soul. Watching Morgan forge metal filled me with a deep sense of completeness and I'm not ashamed to say my eyes were moist as I did so. You see Morgan had not been as 'school clever' as his brother and sister, they'd been wordy and had exam prowess while he'd struggled with the written page although he is innately clever and very witty. His mother however is a very fine ceramic artist and that day at Buscot I realised for the first time that Morgan has his mother's eye and I saw too that Morgan's hands are as eloquent as any words of mine.

Sticks of culture come in many wonderful varieties and as a native of Wales it would be remiss of me not to mention Love Spoons. For centuries young men in Wales would take a stick, look at it long and hard, then begin to carve it into a spoon to troth their love for the girl they admired. Don't think in terms of the wooden spoon we use to stir and sip our cooking for a Love Spoon is a thing of ingenious complication, sometimes with wooden balls in wooden cages all carved out of the single stick. There are written records of them going back to the Sixteenth Century but I'm certain they are a much, much older tradition. To be honest I wouldn't be surprised if the Vikings originally brought them to Wales, as they are quite similar in concept to the Scandinavian Wedding Spoons still presented to brides on their happiest day in Norway and Sweden too.

While we're talking about good and useful sticks we have to mention transport. Many societies did not develop wheel technology and those that did started with solid, wooden affairs. It's been speculated the idea for the wheel came from the turning of pottery wheels that came into being in the Neolithic. Those first cartwheels were heavy, cumbersome affairs until someone had a Eureka moment and inserted some special sticks into the equation. We call them spokes and they were a great leap forward in transport. Lighter and capable of higher speeds they were quickly utilised for warfare in the form of the chariot. However, on the plus side the benefits of the spoke for the carriage of trade has been inestimable.

Our forebears also looked to the water as a route for travel and trade and sticks were vital for the development of river traffic and sea crossings. The first boats were dugout canoes and they still ply the rivers of Asia and South America for relatively short journeys. You can well imagine someone watching a log floating down a river and thinking, "That could get me to the next village in no time." The rest, as they say, is history. But like the solid wooden wheel you can only do so much with a log and humans, with their insatiable curiosity and need to experiment, were soon playing on the water with stick technology. One of the classics is the Native American birch bark canoe made with a framework of sticks, which is ingeniously covered with a single piece of bark from a birch tree sculpted around it. Light, manoeuvrable, easily 'portaged' around rapids it's no wonder the first Europeans to head into the North American interior, trappers in search of furs, enthusiastically took to the water in them.

My favourite stick boats though are to be found in Britain. The first is the type of cross channel ferry I imagine brought the Amesbury Archer to the island's shores; the Dover Boat. I've already mentioned it was quite large enough to make the twenty-mile journey to France and back carrying passengers and a substantial cargo of trade goods. It was a style the experts call a Sewn Plank Boat, constructed of planks of wood hewn with great skill from a tree trunk. But it was the way they were held together that represents a remarkable stick trick. In those times bronze was certainly good for the axes that had revolutionised agriculture by allowing farmers to clear woods off the land in record time.

But nails of bronze weren't so good and our very ingenious forebears came up with a solution. They overlapped the timber boards, drilled holes through them and then lashed them together with withies, which are pliable young willow sticks. Then it was all sealed with pitch and resin before they set sail and it worked wonderfully well. Not so well when experimental archaeologists launched a replica Dover Boat in the town's famous harbour after taking a short cut in the construction. Instead of tree resin and tars they used modern epoxy resins and guess what their retro version sprang multiple leaks within a few minutes. The original, ancient sealant recipe was then applied and lo and behold the cloned Dover Boat sailed admirably well, proving just who knew best out of the Ancient Britons and Modern Boffins. Never spoil a ship for a ha'porth of tar! It lights me up when I think of those truly ancient mariners launching their boat off the beach on the rising tide, loading it with trade goods and helping passengers to embark as the breeze freshened and the continent beckoned. Oh, what an adventure!

There were other styles of sea going boats at that time called Currach, which are still in use on the West Coast of Ireland. Their smaller prehistoric cousin, the coracle, has also survived the ages to still fish for salmon on the rivers of Wales. The Currach was originally made of animal skins stretched over a wooden stick frame and then proofed with pitch; these days they use canvas. They are light and manoeuvrable craft powered by a small sail and oars. On different parts of the coast different Currach evolved to meet local needs so that a boat from Donegal would differ from others. But still they breech the breakers on the Atlantic coast to head for the deep blue ocean as they have done for thousands of years. These days though that's in competitions as Currach racing has become a popular sport on the Irish coast; a testimony to the enduring design skills of our prehistoric ancestors.

In Wales and on the River Spey in Scotland, the Boyne in Ireland too, the boats called coracles, circular in design and notoriously difficult to propel with a single oar, are used for salmon fishing. In Welsh it's called a Corwgl and is constructed in much the same way as the considerably larger Irish Currach. I remember watching the Welsh coracle men of the River Teifi casting nets between two boats in search of salmon. They still go out fishing but these days a shortage of salmon making the run to spawn threatens that way of life. You can buy moulded fibreglass versions of the coracle, which from a distance look entirely authentic, for about £500. Replicas made in China come a bit cheaper. To be fair sportsmen and outdoor enthusiasts are keeping the Coracle tradition alive where the fish are failing and there's a very active Coracle Society. As I write it's run by a British Museum expert called Dr Irving Finkel, Assistant Keeper of the Middle East department, who is famous for decoding a cuneiform tablet detailing the construction of Noah's Ark which apparently was nothing less than a gigantic coracle. Well blow me down.

No less a figure than our old friend Julius Caesar described coracles on the rivers of Britain. So we see the Coracle is obviously a versatile and wonderful craft but did the design reach all the way to America? That's what some people believe and a Coracle enthusiast called Bernard Thomas rowed one across the English Channel in 1974 as part of his campaign to prove the Bull Boats of the Mandan Tribe of North Dakota were copies of coracles. Hang on a minute I hear you say. How the dickens could that have been? Well, there's a school of thought that a North Wales Prince called Madog crossed the Atlantic in a long boat some time in the 12th Century and left some Welsh roots rather like the Vikings before him. There are legends of blue-eyed Natives speaking a language akin to Welsh and President Thomas Jefferson, who had Welsh ancestry, sent out expeditions to find them. Maybe the truth of the legend is still out there somewhere waiting to be discovered. Still, I wonder what the Ancient Britons would have made of a plastic coracle. Who knows, perhaps they'd have liked the non-slip floor? And I think it's entirely fitting that these tiny, obstinate little craft are still navigating the River Boyne in Ireland in sight of so many fantastic Neolithic passage tombs and monuments like those at Newgrange.

Just as salmon take to the air to leap the rapids, eventually so did men and the construction of our earliest flying machines is completely related to that of the Coracle and the Currach. They too were 'stick and skin affairs' with canvas stretched over a frame and, eventually, waterproofed with a gluey substance in a process called 'doping.'

Two Americans, the famous Wright Brothers, Wilbur and Orville, are credited with the first controlled and powered flight in 1903 when they took to the air at Kitty Hawk, North Carolina. What an absolute genie those brothers let out of the bottle and into the world but I'd like to go back a good few centuries to nominate someone else as the father of flight. He's called Eilmer the Flying Monk and he took to the air in a homemade glider around 1005. Eilmer was known as an intellectually brilliant Brother at the Abbey of Malmesbury in Wiltshire, England. A bit of a stargazer he had written extensively about astronomy and the phenomenon of Halle's Comet, which was flaming across the night sky at the time when England was still a Saxon kingdom. It's evident the young monk had a burning curiosity about flight after reading the Greek myths about Icarus and Daedalus flying high towards the sun.

"If they can do it so can I," Eilmer must have thought and he set about making himself some wings. We're not sure of the design but it's generally assumed to be some sort of hang glider with wings attached to his hands and feet; stiffened with sticks. Anyway he took his contraption up to the top of the very tall bell tower of the very wealthy Abbey where he donned his flying suit and took a leap of faith. Many years later William of Malmesbury, a monk at the same Abbey, told the story of Eilmer in a Saxon history, writing:

> *"In his early youth he hazarded a deed of remarkable boldness. He had by some means, I scarcely know what, fastened wings to his hands and feet so that he might fly like Daedalus and, collecting the breeze upon the summit of a tower flew for more than a furlong (six hundred and sixty feet). But agitated by the violence of the wind and the swirling of the air, as well as by the awareness of his rash attempt, he fell, broke both his legs and was lame ever after. He used to relate as the cause of his failure, his forgetting to provide himself with a tail."*

Would you credit it? Even as Eilmer lay in the infirmary with the two legs of his undercarriage broken he was calculating what had gone wrong. "Of course, of course," he told himself, "I encountered some turbulence because I had no stabilising tail!" It's said he approached the Father Abbot, told him there'd been a design failure, informed him he had a better version lined-up and asked permission to have another go. "Not on your life Eilmer, you're grounded," said the Abbot; or words to that effect.

Experts reckon Eilmer would have been in the air for about fifteen seconds, quite long enough I think, and probably landed in a street now called Oliver's Lane; named after him through a mistaken spelling of Oliver for Eilmer. However he has a lasting legacy in a project called Eilmer4 named in his honour at The School of Mechanical and Mining Engineering at the University of Queensland in Australia. According to their website Eilmer4 is, "A program for the simulation of transient, compressible flow in two and three spatial dimensions." Don't ask. I haven't got the foggiest but I have a very strong suspicion that were he alive today, and given an explanation, the first Eilmer would have no problem at all grasping the concept of Eilmer4.

Such is the ubiquitous nature of the stick and I was reminded of more Good Sticks when I was in my local Waitrose store in the town of Marlborough recently chatting to the lovely checkout lady Theresa, who used to be an assistant in the town library. Over the years you get to know the staff at your local store and they become friends, especially in a small market town, so I was telling her about this book.

"Oh, that's marvellous," said Theresa, "I'll never forget when I was a little girl I was watching Blue Peter (a famous children's programme in the UK). Valerie Singleton was the presenter and I can remember being fascinated by the subject. At one time in Chinese culture it was not appropriate for a doctor to physically touch a female patient. So they came up with the idea of having a model of a nude woman made of porcelain and the female patient would point to the place where she was having a problem with a little stick that was provided. They called it a Doctor's Lady and I've never forgotten that."

Fascinating, and quite true, but it has to be said Theresa's example might not be the most efficacious use of sticks in a medical setting. Sticks are of course used in the form of splints to keep broken bones aligned so they might heal. Walking sticks and crutches have been used as 'cripple' supports for thousands of years. Medical staff will routinely use sticks to depress a patient's tongue or to take samples on a swab. Possibly the most game changing piece of medical kit to emerge in the last couple of hundred years is the stethoscope, which allows medics to listen to the goings on inside your chest cavity where the heart and lungs are housed. Frenchman Rene Laennec invented the first stethoscope in 1816 and it was a simple wooden tube. They stayed that way until the end of the nineteenth century when the type we'd recognise was developed.

Perhaps this is a good moment to remind you that the Rod of Asclepius, a stick with a serpent coiled around it, is regarded as the only true symbol of the practice of medicine. Asclepius was, of course, the Greek God of Medicine and Healing. His daughters are appropriately medical too with Hygieia, the goddess of cleanliness, Iaso, goddess of recuperation, Aceso, goddess of the process of healing and Panacea, goddess of the universal remedy.

Good Sticks one and all but when I think of that afternoon back home in Wales watching those boats built of sticks, the coracles of the River Teifi, I feel a bewildering blend of happiness and foreboding. Below the waterfalls at Cenarth two boats moved like beetles on the surface, their flat bottoms skimmed along by flat-capped men weaving broad leafed oars in the river. The backs of the salmon flashed in beams of sunlight, as they headed upstream to leap the falls while a myriad midges floated like motes in the light above them. And the rocks were all glistening, not from the spray, but from a million tiny young eels wriggling their way around the cascade as they followed the fish upstream. I was a little boy holding my mother's hand. I'll never do that again and I fear none of us will ever see another host of tiny elvers migrating up a British river; not in my lifetime I'm sure.

Chapter 9
MAGIC STICKS

It was a warm spring day, in fact it was Mayday 2007, and I was sitting on a wall above a house on one of the steep lanes that twist like fishing lines to converge on the harbour side at Padstow in Cornwall. Sitting next to me enjoying the sunshine was my friend Kate Merry, sister of Alex the esteemed illustrator of this book. Kate and me were listening to the growing sound of a drum and accordion band coming our way from the big manor house at Prideaux Place on the hill above. I'd joined Kate and a group of her friends who are all contemporaries of my eldest son Harry and she'd been his housemate for years.

It's always good to meet up with Kate to feel her special, creative energy but that day was different because it was the first time either of us had been to watch the peculiarly Cornish Mayday celebration of the Obby Oss. It goes like this. The town is decorated with flowers and a giant Maypole erected overnight, there's a lot of singing and then in the morning the accordion bands emerge from the confines of the pub to begin their daylong repetition of the same song, the same rhythmic drumming, to welcome in the days of summer. It's then the Obby Oss emerges from his 'stable' in the pub. That day we'd missed the start of proceedings and were waiting for the procession to come into sight while the music spilled down the hill ahead of it. Men and women, fishing folk, lifeboat crew, nurses, shop workers; chefs and IT consultants for all I know. Every trade and calling in Padstow is in the mix as they drill the rhythm and squeeze out the melody for the Oss but all of them have to be local folk.

And then, and then, the Oss came into sight and my heart took flight as a great disc of lacquered wood, with a horse's tail, a mane and a ghastly pointed head, spun round and round like the disc of the heavens in a potent dance. Underneath a strong young man bearing the Oss is trying to capture a maid beneath the folds of a skirt around the hoop. All around the Oss a flock of girls dance the steps they'll dance all day, hop, step and skip in a Cornish sort of way as they sing the song that again and again they'll sing all day. Fragments of it understood...*Unite and ...For summer is acome unto day...In the merry morning of May.*

Suddenly the Oss collapses, lying prone and the song takes a different, sombre turn until he resurrects and joy infuses the tune again. All the while a stick conducts proceedings, it's a wand with a padded heart held in the hand of the Oss's teaser, a role played in turn by young and old alike; boys and girls, men and women. It's an ancient rite the Obby Oss. I felt that in my bones, perhaps re-invented in Victorian times with accordions thrown in for good measure. But it's roots lie in the deep Celtic past of the Cornish people and everything about it roared at me, 'this is all about community!' The procession passed us by, Kate, her friends and me, as it revolved around the town again and I looked at Kate, the look returned, both of us eyes brimming with tears.

I've been back to Padstow on Mayday twice since with Stephanie and each time we've felt the same intensity; the same overpowering sense of community. These days there are two Oss processions, the Red and the Blue, which was formed in memory of those Padstow men who fell in the Great War. That's real community for you and I've felt this strong welling of place before, back home in Wales among my own folk. The people of Padstow don't need to explain any of this of course. For them it's nothing less than a deeply felt, natural phase of the year when they all join together to celebrate what the place under their feet means to them. There are other Oss celebrations in Cornwall and a couple in Devon and Dorset, not so far away, and to give weight to the Oss's antiquity there is a very similar manifestation in Wales called the Mari Lwyd; originally a celebration of the horse goddess Rhiannon, known to the Celtic Gauls as Great Epona. But it's the Padstow Oss that takes the Crown.

Oh, the magic of sticks. Not hard to find in nature. Just cut a branch of willow then trim it off and point the end before you plunge it into the ground. Come back in the spring and it will have struck roots and grown and not for nothing is it called a willow wand. And it's that miracle of stick regeneration that gave rise to one of England's sacred Christian myths in the Glastonbury Thorn, which flowers every Christmas and is said to have been planted by Christ's great-uncle, Joseph of Aramethea.

Did Joseph plant the thorn bush? I doubt it. More likely the ever-inventive monks of Glastonbury came up with the story to encourage the tourist trade, which in those days essentially comprised pilgrims. They had after all conveniently found King Arthur's grave on their land, which turned into a bit of a tourist gold mine. Did Joseph ever visit Glastonbury? I feel that's far more likely as in Roman times Britain was a valuable source of mineral wealth; particularly Cornish tin. But there was also a huge Roman lead mining project in the Mendip hills just a few miles from Glastonbury, near Cheddar, and we know from history that Joseph was a metal trader certified by the Emperor himself. Glastonbury, the legendary Isle of Avalon, was just twelve miles from the sea across a vast expanse of wetlands and probably navigable from the Bristol Channel at the time. So why wouldn't Joseph come to western Britain in search of a profitable deal for Somerset lead? I like to think he did.

No miracle thorn bush but there are other sticks that display a magical propensity that science just can't explain and they're called Dowsing Sticks. Usually cut from hazel these Y shaped prongs have been used by mankind for centuries to 'divine' the presence of water or valuable minerals under the surface of the ground. These days they're also used to trace the course of natural power lines called ley lines. Is this just hippy hogwash or New Age nonsense? I'm certain dowsing is neither. Years ago I lived in a house that lay on the most famous of the ley lines the Michael Line, which runs through the spine of the West Country. It was our local postman Roland who introduced me to the Michael Line in the most serendipitous of ways. I'd just driven home from an assignment and as I turned the corner there was Roland outside my house with an L-shaped copper rod in each hand. The handle of each rod was held in a plastic tube so that it could freely move but could not be turned this way or that by the user's hand.

"What's going on?" I asked.

"Well," said Roland the Postman, "I've just dowsed the width of the Michael Line on the lane but it runs right through your house, directly through the kitchen between your AGA cooker and the microwave. About nine or ten feet wide."

Blimey! The AGA and the microwave; who knew! I didn't realise but Roland had already marked out the width of the Line on the road with a couple of stones. He asked if I wanted to try so I took the rods into my hands and walked towards the house when suddenly the two rods moved to point inwards. I kept moving forward and then after nine or ten feet they shot out again. Only then did Roland show me the marker stones he'd placed on the ground to show my wife and my mother-in-law who were watching. They were at the exact spots where the rods had moved.

Not content with that dramatic demonstration Roland asked me to walk round the corner to the ancient local church; one of the few in the country that has a Neolithic round barrow burial site in its graveyard. We climbed fifteen feet or so to the top of the barrow. Roland held the rods out and they started to whirl around at speed like the rotors of a helicopter. That happened, he explained, because barrows were often put up at places where a number of ley lines intersect. I was impressed however Roland told me his copper rods were quite showy but he'd prefer to use a Y shaped hazel dowsing stick any day. I haven't seen Roland about for a while and I can only hope that he's well and dowsing still. At any rate he'd convinced me ley lines exist and the power of dowsing is a real one. To be honest the verified examples of successful dowsing expeditions are too numerous to catalogue in a book like this. Just to say that dowsers, mostly from Germany, were employed in the 16th Century to find rich veins of tin in the Cornish mines and to strike silver in the mines of Mid Wales too.

But there's one example of the skills of a dowser so amazing I'd like to repeat it here. I watched it unfold on television about thirty years ago and remember being bowled over by what I saw. First I must tell you about the Isles of Scilly, an archipelago of beautiful islands lying in the warming current of the Gulf Stream about twenty miles off Lands End. In the Bronze Age the string of several islands that exist today were largely one mass until a global warming event saw a twenty or thirty metre rise in sea levels which inundated the low lying parts of that land mass creating what we see today.

The flood drowned numerous Bronze Age communities on Scilly leaving archaeological remains that have since been catalogued by marine archaeologists. However around ten times a year on average the tides are low enough to allow people to walk across the once-upon-a-time, drowned land of fabled Lyonesse between the islands of Bryher and Tresco. That's where the dowsing came in and I remember watching that TV programme with an expert dowser from the mainland standing on the deck of one of the launches that serve as ferries between the islands. He was holding his Y shaped branch of hazel. He reckoned to have found a freshwater spring through the wooden deck of the boat and thirty feet of running seawater beneath.

The location was carefully charted and then the group involved waited until the big low tide saw the sea rush out and leave the land between Bryher and Tresco exposed again. They included some independent witnesses, who went to the location and sure enough they found a freshwater spring, which must have been used by the Bronze Age folk who once lived there. Truly incredible and all the more so when you learn the dowser had never been to the Isles of Scilly Isles before. Okay, whilst I clearly remember the programme, not least because I was a regular visitor to the Islands at the time, I couldn't recall any of the finer detail; importantly not the name of the dowser himself. So I reached out by e-mail to Jill Moss of Trencrom Dowsers, a group based in West Cornwall. Jill also runs the Penwith Press, a publishing group dedicated to all things dowsing including ley lines and other earth power theories.

Jill was kindness personified and inquired of her contacts including Ba Miller, widow of a famous dowser called Hamish Miller. Jill e- mailed me back telling me she'd had a chance to speak with Ba who remembered the dowsing adventure I'd described and said it had been done by a well known water dowser called Donovan Wilkins, who died in 2015. Jill's e-mail continued:

> *"Incidentally, a freshwater spring has also been found at the side of St Michael's Mount - logical really as both the Mount and Scilly were part of the mainland not so long ago."*

Then in a subsequent mail Jill urged me not to label dowsing, as 'magic' as she contends there is nothing the least bit magic about it. Jill told me she and her husband John believed dowsing is a skill that can be learnt with practice and is absolutely not a gift. She also thought it unfortunate that in English we use the word 'divining', which has helped develop an unnecessary mystique and suspicion around the subject. Well, I thought, I don't like to disagree with someone as agreeable as Jill but to my mind there's nothing prosaic about dowsing at all. Jill publishes dowsing literature and is leader of an active dowsing group so my immediate thoughts were sorry Jill the way I see it you're on the inside looking out whilst from my perspective something science can offer no plausible explanation for seems pretty magical. And then I got another, revelatory e-mail from Jill, which entirely explained the dowsing community's sensitivities about the word 'magic' in connection with their ancient craft. Here it is:

> *"Dowsing/divining was declared illegal under the Witchcraft Act of 1562, (there were several of these Acts) and remained that way until the Act was repealed in 1951! It then came within the remit of the Fraudulent Mediums Act and then in 2008 was taken under the wing of the Consumer Services Act. At that time John, (then Director of the British Society of Dowsers) met with MEPs to ensure that dowsing did not slip back into the witchcraft era.*

> *Despite it being illegal, dowsing was clearly taking place through the centuries in the search for water and minerals. An engraving in the 16thC book 'De Re Metallica' shows dowsers at work with forked sticks, and miners busy digging alongside them. In addition, Elizabeth I imported German dowsers to help with the search for minerals, a much-needed resource."*

Unbelievable. Dowsing was still being lumped in with all the other superstitious garbage about witchcraft when I was two years of age a few years after the end of World War II. The perception of the miraculous associated with dowsing had led the Church to condemn it. After all the only miracles the Church could countenance were those linked to the name of Christ, the Virgin Mary or the Saints. A local bloke going into the countryside and finding a vein of silver with a stick could do nothing but seriously devalue the currency of Church sanctified miracles. Ban it!

It certainly explained where Jill's coming from and the name for dowsing in the American Appalachians, where it's called Water Witching, would definitely feed into her concerns. There are fundamentalists from all the major book-based religions who'd be only too keen to start witch-hunts again given half a chance. I thought about it a lot and eventually decided to accept what Jill says. Anyone can dowse and after all hadn't I successfully dowsed the Michael Line after a fashion myself. What then explains this enigmatic practice? Of, course it's the hazel stick that holds the magic and not the person wielding it. With that in mind I'm going to have a T-shirt printed emblazoned with the words: 'Dowsing Sticks are Magic.'

Time to move on to an altogether racier sort of stick and that's the Witches Broomstick. I mentioned them in the Sporty Stick chapter in relation to those officiandos who play the Harry Potter game Quidditch; chasing a ball around with a broom between their legs. Well, I'm not sure how much J. K. Rowling knew about the source of the broom-flying phenomenon of witchcraft when she wrote her famous books but here goes.

Very few people buy into the idea that witches could actually fly on their brooms and I certainly don't know any who do. What was, and for all I know, still is happening was the use of natural psychotropic drugs to bring about a kind of out of body experience. In this way exponents of witchcraft were indeed, at least to their minds, flying around the countryside. And to achieve this astral effect they used various unguents applied to the skin known as 'flying ointments' or 'witches ointments.' To put it in common parlance they weren't flying, they were tripping.

Most historians, chemists and modern witches list the ingredients as a collection of some seriously toxic plants such as Deadly Nightshade, Henbane, Mandrake, Hemlock and Wolfsbane; the list is a long one and varies with the climate of a particular region. They can be taken orally but witches discovered early on best not for the sake of your tummy but no worries they can also be taken transdermally. In other words if they're rubbed on the skin the active ingredients will pass through into the blood stream taking their psychotropic alkaloids with them rather like the Novichok nerve agents the Russians used in their infamous assassination attacks in the otherwise genteel Cathedral City of Salisbury in 2018.

The main chemical agents in flying ointments listed by the experts are atropine, hyoscyamine and scopolamine, the so-called truth drug first used by the Nazi Gestapo for interrogations. It's worth noting too that witchcraft's many enemies claimed the whole concoction was rounded off with 'the fat of children digged out of their graves' and other loathsome ingredients. This is reflected in the famous lines of Shakespeare's witches in Macbeth who stirred their cauldron on the blasted heath while incanting the recipe for their foul brew. It went like this:

'In the caldron boil and bake;
Eye of newt and toe of frog,
Wool of bat and tongue of dog,
Adder's fork and blind-worm's sting,
Lizard's leg and howlet's wing,
For a charm of powerful trouble,
Like a hell-broth boil and bubble.'

Gruesome stuff but I think Shakespeare very nearly hit on something here even if he was a lizard's leg and a frog's toe short of the mark. In his day I suspect the inns and hostelries of England would have been full of scary, witch gossip; they would have been the terrifying zombie apocalypse horror tales of the time. And Shakespeare probably heard some witchy stuff about the amphibians' parts they used in their spells whispered over a pot of ale. But he got the wrong creature. Will would have been nearer the mark if his witches' spell had gone something like: "Eye of newt and skin of toad."

That's because the Common Toad, Latin name Bufo Bufo, contains a powerful hallucinogenic in its skin designed to deter predators. It's called buffoteine and can be ingested into the human system through the skin and I'm not alone in thinking witches were boiling up toads in their brews and skimming off the hallucinogenic lard for their flying ointments. Okay, we've boiled up our Deadly Nightshade together with our toad skins and skimmed off our pot of fatty ointment but how do we use it? Well, smearing it over the skin might be the simplest of the options but there were said to be other, more direct delivery systems favoured by witches. At this point I recommend those of you with delicate sensibilities should scan over the next several lines until you detect the word 'armpit' and resume reading again.

Like it or not the witches broom is a powerful phallic symbol and the evidence of the use of sex toys to deliver flying ointments into the system through the vagina has come down the centuries in repeated anecdotes from all over Europe. There is however one extraordinary case that makes the same point in the historical transcripts of a 14th Century witch trial in Ireland. Alice Kyteler was a Norman Irish gentlewoman from Kilkenny who was extremely wealthy and apparently very beautiful and quite libidinous too. Importantly she'd been a moneylender and had also owned an inn near Kilkenny famed for the beauty of its serving girls; a place frequented by the rich and powerful of the day. Alice's history was somewhat chequered to say the least and in her wake it was alleged she left a couple of poisoned husbands, disinherited a few stepchildren and had a satanic familiar called Robert son of Art, who she summoned from the depths of hell to be her lover.

It has to be said that even in the absence of any witchcraft allegations folk in those times didn't like rumours about murdered husbands and the brewing of poisons. Poisoning has always been considered a particularly loathsome crime so one thing led to another and gossip turned into accusation until the local Bishop joined in to raise witchcraft as a possibility. However Alice was politically influential and, reading between the lines, I suspect that may have been because she had a lot of dirt on the local nobility who'd frolicked with the local beauties at her inn at Kilkenny. Maybe a few of the Norman toffs owed the beautiful moneylender some cash too. In any event a local power struggle between the Church and Irish dignitaries ensued, which actually saw the Bishop locked up for a couple of weeks. It wasn't enough to protect Alice though as the allegations became overwhelming when her maid Petronilla of Meath confessed and implicated Alice under torture. Alice bought herself a passage out of Ireland and was never seen again although she was tried in her absence and both she and the unfortunate Alice were sentenced to burn at the stake.

Where does the flying ointment come into all this you may ask? Well, according to the court records when officials were sent to search or 'rifle' Dame Alice's house they found *"a wafer of sacramental bread having the devil's name stamped thereon and a pipe of ointment wherewith she greased a staffe upon which she ambled and galloped through thick and thin, when and in what manner she listed."*

In plain language they found witches' unguents and a sex toy, which Alice had used to apply her psychotropic lube internally before making love with her familiar and flying across the skies of her mind to join the coven. A wealthy woman might have possessed such sophisticated apparatus; who's to say poorer witches didn't have to avail themselves instead of a broomstick with a handle worn smooth through regular housework?

I've read a lot of material about this trial including tracts by modern witches feigning horror, in surprisingly puritanical terms, that a sex toy would be used for this purpose. I find that quite puzzling and simply pose the question, why not? The evidence is there. Anecdotal accounts from across Europe abound but the Dame Alice case is much plainer. There are protestations that it came under torture but that's not quite true. Unlike her maid Alice was never tortured and the discoveries made by the officials who ransacked her house seem conclusive not least because of the support offered Alice by powerful men. No less a person than the local Chancellor was among them and that would definitely have deterred any minor court lackey from planting the evidence.

One point has to be made strongly here. There is no justification whatsoever for witchcraft trials or burning people at the stake for the pretty harmless crime of playing out drug-induced, phantasmagorical journeys and love trysts in the privacy of their own homes. Indeed the term witch-hunt has since come to mean an unjustified attempt to convict innocent people. If Alice had been convicted of poisoning one or other of her husbands that would have been a different matter. As it was she let her maid take the rap and it was poor Petronilla who died in the flames calling for Alice to come to her aid right up to the end. They would have piled bundles of faggots around the maid and set light to them to bring her to an horrific end. How much happier an outcome if some latter day river keeper like John Hounslow had dragged those faggots away from the execution pyre and used them to improve a riverbank. And therein lies the paradox of sticks for you. The same sticks can be used for good or evil; arranged to enhance the banks of a river or lit to burn a poor 'witch' at the stake. If I may, one last point about magic broomsticks. Other sources from the medieval cite the armpits as a good place to spread your flying ointment and I just want to say that if I were of a warlock's disposition I would definitely be an armpit man.

Abracadabra! Let's leave the fetid world of the broomstick behind and look at that quintessentially magical stick, the wand. Wands have been intricately entwined with the works of magicians, sorcerers, wizards, necromancers and kindly fairy godmothers throughout the history of fiction. To this day they seem to feature in every evocation of magic be it on stage, screen or on the pages of books. We see wands everywhere flashing out bolts of lightning in duals between good wizards and bad; turning people into pigs or a pumpkin into a carriage for the ball.

One of my favourite wands was the one wielded by that wonderful British comedian Tommy Cooper in his comically, error-strewn magician's act. His wand called down gales of laughter rather than bolts of lightning and all the better for that. In the Harry Potter adventures the wands choose their owners but I'm pretty certain Tommy Cooper chose his own. There are too many magical adventure stories and too many mind-boggling magicians' acts, where a wand is the essential prop, to mention. And sadly in these days of terror attacks a wand has also come to describe the electronic metal detector that's run over a person at a security gate in search of weapons.

Another magical stick, one that's sometimes called a wand, is the conductors' baton. I have no idea how this works being unmusical as well as innumerate but it's a source of wonder to me that a couple of dozen pairs of eyes or more can watch the movement of a stick through the air then mimic that movement in beautiful sounds. And while we're talking about the sticks that translate the fire of man's imagination what about the paint brushes used by great artists? I'm not just talking about those masters we recognize in the catalogue of classics from the Renaissance or the great thematic schools of more recent centuries. To my mind there's surely no great divide between Michelangelo painting by candlelight on the cavernous ceiling of the Sistine Chapel or the hunter-gatherer genius who made his or her way deep into a cave at Altamira to conjure images of deer and buffalo upon the cavern wall by the flickering glow of a torch. Michelangelo used brushes loaded with hair while our cave artist etched with a spear point then applied colours with straw, moss, leaves and sometimes hair on a stick describing the beloved prey with unutterable beauty.

Magic wands of sorts indeed and who'd deny it but where does the concept of the magic wand actually have its origins? Some say its basis lies in the phallic symbol, others that it was taken from a shaman's drumstick long, long ago. I don't think so. I believe I've heard a far more powerful, spine tingling explanation that lies in that period of cultural explosion on the cusp of the Bronze Age. Some years ago I was researching a novel, it's a time shift story partly set in the Bronze Age; a period you might already have guessed that fascinates me. During this research I had some odd, repeated dreams about a boy stirring a vat of steaming liquid. Hold onto that for a little while if you would, while I tell you more because it was then that I saw an article about an archaeological phenomenon known as a 'Burnt Mound.'

Burnt Mounds are relatively common features from the Bronze Age their presence revealed by a pile of fire-charred boulders lying in a roughly crescent shape close to what had once been a buried wooden coffer designed to hold many gallons of liquid. These human constructs are invariably found close to a stream and often the vestiges of a launder, or wooden chute, to draw off water into the coffer is present too. Over the years there's been a great deal of speculation among archaeologists about the purpose of these enigmatic structures. Were they saunas, perhaps for ritual bathing, or were they more mundane communal cooking facilities? No one could be certain.

The Burnt Mound I first read about was at a place called Hell's Bay on the Lleyn Peninsula in North Wales and experimental archaeologists from a group called Ancient Arts, led by David Chapman, had decided to make their own assemblage and test the theory that these constructions might actually have been Bronze Age Breweries. Two Irish archaeologists, Billy Quinn and Declan Moore, had first put this theory to the test and to be fair Dave Chapman had fulsomely acknowledged this before he began his experiment. However there was certainly no harm in testing the theory a second time in a different location.

Ancient Arts built an oak coffer a quarter the size of the original then sealed it with clay before filling it with water and collecting a large pile of stones over which they lit a fire. When the stones turned white at maximum temperature they were raked from the fire and dropped into the coffer to boil the water until it was sterilized. Then they added malted barley to the hot water to create what is known as a brewer's wort, which they let suppurate for an hour and a half at a constant heat by adding a fresh, hot stone every ten minutes. As they worked they discovered that the classic horseshoe or crescent shape of Burnt Mounds appeared naturally as the archaeologists instinctively used the most ergonometrically efficient way of removing and stacking the used stones to cool.

Elderberry skins are the richest source of natural yeast known in Northern Europe so the team threw elderberries in the mix as well as honey, blackberries and rosehips for flavour but no magic mushrooms as it's thought the ancients did. Hot, hard work by the sounds but they had to let their Bronze Age brew ferment for a few days before they were rewarded with seventy seven pints of palatable beer and a barley mash that was baked into tasty biscuits as a bonus. What a wonderful experiment and a pretty convincing one as they were left with some of the tell tale signatures of the original Burnt Mounds they were investigating.

It seems brewing was indeed the answer but as I mentioned Billy Quinn and Declan Moore, had come up with the theory first and had also done the first re-creation of a Bronze Age brewery at Billy's home in Cordarragh, County Galway producing: *"A relatively clear, copper-coloured brew with a distinctively sharp yet sweet taste. The hot rocks impart a slightly smoky caramelized character. In short it was nice!"*

There were a few differences in approach and detail between the Hell's Bay re-creation and the Irish one but the conclusion had been the same; it was for brewing. However there was also a difference in emphasis as the Moore Group's 'fulacht fiadhs' as these ancient breweries are known in Ireland produced one hundred and ten litres of their Bronze Age brand against the miserly seventy-seven pints in Wales. It has to be said there's an emerging theme here. We all know the Irish enjoy a beer and I mean that as a compliment and so far some four thousand five hundred 'fulacht fiadhs' have been identified in Bronze Age Ireland making it, as Declan points out with more than a hint of unscientific pride, 'the most widespread brewing industry in pre-history.' Cheers Declan and Billy! Or should I say 'Slainte!'

Where then is the magic wand in all this you may ask and here's the part that makes me pause to wonder at all that shapes us from our ancestors and all that makes us who we are. You see, you have to use a stick to stir the wort and once the elderberries have been added and the yeast is in the mix your stick will be imbued with the life- giving cells of the fermenting microbe. And then the living, sticky slime on your stick will set the next brew alive as you stir it, as if by magic. Declan Moore and Billy Quinn clearly seem to have been enchanted by this and proposed a theory that set my spine tingling. They concluded these magical sticks or wands covered with a residue impregnated with the living yeast cells would have been potent spiritual symbols. And as a shaman would undoubtedly have presided over the brewing then the effect on those watching would have been no less powerful than that of 'Christ's miraculous changing of water into wine.'

It was 2009 when I first read those thrilling words in Declan and Billy's theory and it immediately made sense of my recurring dreams of a boy stirring a steaming vat and so I began my novel The Golden Cape. It became a struggle as other book projects and a three-year battle with the effects of Lyme Disease greedily consumed my time but in the end I finished the work. Inspired, as it was by my own dreams and by undreamt of wands drawn from the archaeological runes of Ireland by Declan Moore and Billy Quinn. In the novel my young hero Gwion says this:

> *'My hazel switch was still quick with the yeasty slime of the last brew as I stood above the trough to work my sorcery. The sterile trough began to brew at once and there I stood waving my hazel switch across the wort. It was a stick no more but a wand that let me carry magic in my hand."*

And so the hope in my heart is that I've waved my switch across your life and helped you to divine the magic of sticks in all their many guises and to show how they've blessed and cursed our kind in equal measure. I hope too you'll share with me a sense of wonder at the astonishing variety of sticks that have lined the route of mankind's history. Fuel, shelter, weapons, measurement, the symbols of our spirituality and culture, even the supernatural arrows of Orion's belt, all are sourced from sticks. Sticks gave us the yeast-blessed wand of the ancient brewer and they gave us the humble weaving shuttle; a stick propelled back and forth with an efficiency so cosmically simple it lends its name to spacecraft that hurtle astronauts to the edge of the stars and back. Sticks.

THE END

*****

THE AUTHOR

Alun Rees was born in Wales where he began his award winning career as a journalist on the South Wales Echo before joining the Daily Mail then the Daily Express. He covered assignments around the world before taking up the role of West Country correspondent for the Daily Express. For the past ten years he's been a freelance journalist and co-author of best selling military non-fiction including Highway to Hell, Spearhead Assault. He also co-wrote the Be a Hero: The Essential Survival Guide to Active-Shooter Events.

He lives on the banks of the River Kennet near Marlborough, Wiltshire and is a keen amateur naturalist and his winter pastime is working his three gundogs on local shoots.

THE ILLUSTRATOR

Alex Merry lives in Stroud, Gloucestershire, and studied Illustration at the University of the West of England. She has worked for Damien Hirst at his studios near Stroud and lately produced a number of illustrations for Gucci Interiors, which were translated into giant murals on the walls of buildings in Hong Kong, Milan, Shanghai, New York and London. Alex also completed the stunning series of archway murals for the Gucci Garden project featured in Vogue International.

Beside her love of art, Alex's passion is Morris Dancing and she's a member of the flamboyant, cutting edge group Boss Morris who perform at festivals and with top bands. Her father is a retired Vicar and her mother, brother and sister are all successful artists.

38445892R00099

Printed in Poland
by Amazon Fulfillment
Poland Sp. z o.o., Wrocław